MATURING with MOXIE

Jan Cannon

MATURING
WITH MOXIE

A WOMAN'S GUIDE TO LIFE AFTER 60

ForeEdge

ForeEdge
An imprint of University Press of New England
www.upne.com
© 2018 ForeEdge
All rights reserved
Manufactured in the United States of America
Designed by Mindy Basinger Hill
Typeset in Fresco Pro

For permission to reproduce any of the material in this book, contact
Permissions, University Press of New England,
One Court Street, Suite 250, Lebanon NH 03766; or visit
www.upne.com

Library of Congress Cataloging-in-Publication Data

Names: Cannon, Jan, author.

Title: Maturing with moxie: a woman's guide to life after 60 / Jan Cannon.

Description: Lebanon, NH: ForeEdge, [2018] | Includes bibliographical
references and index.

Identifiers: LCCN 2017050829 (print) | LCCN 2017053576 (ebook) |
ISBN 9781512602791 (epub, mobi, & pdf) | ISBN 9781512602784 (pbk.)

Subjects: LCSH: Older women—Life skills guides. | Aging.

Classification: LCC HQ1061 (ebook) | LCC HQ1061. C3324 2018 (print) |
DDC 305.26/2—dc23

LC record available at https://lccn.loc.gov/2017050829

5 4 3 2 1

TO MY ROLE MODELS Helen Troescher (1897–1988), Helen Bond (1915–1992), Miriam Smith (1919–2000), Jean Chapin Smith (1930–2015), Louise Ambler (1934–), and Joyce Mehring (1937–)

CONTENTS

PREFACE

On average, if you're 60 today, you can expect to live to 85.
—Social Security Life Expectancy Calculator

When I turned sixty, I wondered if I had become "a woman of a certain age"—or did that occur at sixty-five? Then I became a grandmother and again wondered if I'd passed into another category where I might suddenly have to wear black shoes with laces, as my grandmothers did. But then I realized it was up to me to define who I was—and who I would become.

I looked for guides, both people and books, and I found only partial answers. Some told me what my financial needs and goals for retirement should be. Others guided me to leisure and volunteer activities. Friends extolled the virtues of "early-bird" dining and senior discounts on everything from movie tickets to property tax reductions. But nowhere and no one provided a comprehensive guide to the changes ahead in this, my so-called "third age" (although it might really be called a "fifth age" after childhood, the teen years, young adulthood, and middle age—whenever that ended).

I don't think of myself as old, as in "old age." That will come in my late eighties when I plan to be alternately disagreeable and sweet. And I'm certainly not a "senior citizen," although I do take advantage of any senior discounts I'm eligible for (including coffee at fast food chains). And I'm clearly not part of the silver-haired league, since my natural strawberry-blonde locks are just starting to show streaks of platinum (or, less poetically, white).

I take yoga classes and visit the gym regularly (well, okay, not *every* day). I grow pots of tomatoes on my small deck and try to eat a healthy diet, but will admit to sometimes having a "dinner" of cheese and crackers with a glass or two of red wine. My blood pressure and cholesterol are not being medicated, although they have been and might be again. (I've worked hard to lose forty pounds I really didn't need. But there are no promises that they won't somehow find their way back.) So all the advice I've read for a healthy old age is just more of the same, as far as I'm concerned. Mind you, that's not bad. I just find it a little limited.

This is all just to say that I haven't found a guide that looks at the financial, health, social, *and* emotional issues of being older. Why is this important? Because each topic affects the others, either positively or negatively, in creating a sense of happiness and fulfillment. Since I couldn't find that guidebook, I decided to write it—as a resource for other people like me: older, but not old (yet), looking for help with the new realities of our lives. It's designed as a starting place to answer questions about living well at any age. *Maturing with Moxie: A Woman's Guide to Life after 60* addresses the challenges of aging with gusto and doing something positive to make life enjoyable, instead of merely endurable.

Every stage of life requires balancing competing goals; enhancing skills; adapting to the current political, social, and economic realities; and finding your own unique path through shared generational challenges. I've spent over twenty years as a career adviser, coach, and workshop leader helping others discover their paths. This book is the result of applying the same process to my own decisions and finding some common themes in my own and others' strategies for dealing with the demands of this stage of life. I researched each of the topics included in this book, gathering the information I discovered from many sources into one place. Instead of four or five books addressing only some of the critical topics for decision-making in the decades after age sixty, this one book is a resource covering them all.

The following chapters contain stories of people living the lives they want. Their examples, along with a wealth of information and resources, will help you get started designing your own future. This book will help you learn about housing options, so you don't have to worry about living on the street. It will also help you face the issue of money—including insurance, Social Security, retirement plans, budgets, and debt management. In the social realm, you will learn how to meet new people, maybe even a new partner. Good health, of course, is key to having fun. So there's a section on lifestyle and how to pick a new doctor, a younger one interested in aging, of course. Part of being healthy is keeping the brain as fully functional as possible; that means learning new things and being in new situations. And what guide to aging would be complete without mention of family matters? You might now be head of the clan, or still caring for a parent, child, grandchild, sibling, or other loved one. Perhaps you and a spouse or partner are spending more time together. There are helpful hints to make this all manageable—and maybe even fun.

Write in the margins, underline sentences, fill out the checklists—make this a tool to take on the journey to a fabulous old age. You'll meet fellow travelers whose examples may give you new ideas for your own life. I've learned a lot while compiling the information in the following pages, and I've met some amazing folks along the way who helped me see new possibilities. I hope this book will help you find the answers to living well into the decades ahead.

ACKNOWLEDGMENTS

Many thanks to my tolerant writing group—Joani Mountain, Pat O'Brien, and Blythe Sterling—who read early versions of this tome again and again. And to my cheerleaders, Nancy Hammett and Kathryn Kay, who kept reminding me that I needed to get this finished so they could use the information. Special thanks to my first readers, Alice Poltorick, Anne Rosen, Dianne Hobbs, and Ginny Rohan, for their valuable feedback. The technical assistance from Laurie Ruskin and Chris Daly was much appreciated. And the entire project would not be possible without the enthusiastic encouragement of my editors, Phyllis Deutsch, Susan Abel, and Amanda Dupuis. My gratitude to all of you for being doulas to this project.

I have changed the names and some details in order to preserve the privacy of those who generously shared their stories with me.

MATURING with MOXIE

1 MATURING WITH MOXIE

mox·ie ['mɑksi] n. slang. energy; spunk; spirit:
What he lacked in experience or education, he made up for in moxie.
—*Dictionary of American Slang and Colloquial Expressions*

What does it mean to mature with moxie? It means you're ready to take charge and guide your life rather than let circumstances guide you. In other words:

Live well until you die!

Take risks!

Focus on action and passion!

Make plans—but be willing to change them!

When you mature with moxie, you've chosen to live life to the fullest, have fun, and greet new opportunities and change with optimism.

This book is a guide to help you do that.

As baby boomers, we don't think of ourselves as old—it's not our style. But we are aging, and models of aging from the past may not always apply. We can decide how we're going to face the challenges ahead. The people you'll meet in the following pages have done just that—and I hope you'll let their experiences and their stories inspire you.

We've been a generation that redefined every passage: we were hippies and demonstrators in our twenties, civil rights and women's lib advocates in our thirties; we experienced midlife crises in our forties, became empty-nesters in our fifties, and now we're leading the way into a new passage that has no name (yet). We had passion for our causes and we changed the way we approached our work, our families, our communities, and the environment along the way. We are Vietnam vets and antiwar protesters, flower children, and corporate cogs à la *Mad Men*. We married young, got divorced, and—maybe—married again. Some of us moved in with one another and never married, maybe because, as same-sex partners, we weren't allowed to by law. We've discussed birth control, menopause, and erectile dysfunction as easily as the weather and last night's box scores. And it's not over yet.

Our sources of wisdom have changed. Before the publication of Dr. Benjamin Spock's *The Common Sense Book of Baby and Child Care* in 1946, child-rearing techniques were passed on from one generation to the next by individuals. This was easy because we lived in close proximity to one another. But the rise to dominance of the nuclear family and the move to the suburbs generally meant less contact with elder relatives and more contact with peers who often didn't have a stock of wisdom and experience to share. Without experienced elders close at hand, the next best thing was a guide to raising babies—a book—and Dr. Spock was there. Today, once again, we're at the vanguard of change as more and more people are living well into their eighties and nineties. We're different from our parents (and our children), and until now we haven't had a guidebook to tell us how to deal with that. This is it.

Maturing with Moxie will show you a range of options for aging well. It will present new chances to reinvent yourself, to take the risks or make the changes you never thought possible when you were paying a mortgage or educating yourself or your children. You were *responsible* back then, and maybe even a little *boring*. Now, at this new stage of life, you can be the butterfly emerging from a cocoon of experience, transformed and ready to fly. I know this can happen, because it's happened to me and to the people whose stories are shared in the following chapters. Their stories will show you what's possible. But your story will be uniquely yours.

If I can do it, so can you. Let me tell you a little about how I got here. I'm not from a privileged background—both of my parents were teachers. And I never had a high-paying job. I think my highest annual earnings were $45,000 in 1992. But I've managed, even thrived, because I took charge of my life when I could. And that is what I want to encourage you to do, too.

I don't remember being a risk taker as a child—except for climbing into the swaying branches of the maple tree in the front yard of my suburban Cleveland home. I went to school, did my homework, and played with the neighborhood kids. I sold Girl Scout cookies and went to day camp and high school football games. It all seemed pretty ordinary.

I learned to ski as a twenty-something. I had no idea what I was getting myself into. It was a lot harder than it looked on TV. Long boards attached to your feet are not so easy to rearrange after an ungainly plop onto hard-packed snow, no matter how athletic you think you are. The fact that I kept up with it for enough winters that my kids and I would take ski vacations into their teens is either a testimony to my moxie or a proof of stubborn stupidity. I'd like to credit the moxie. Since I've now broken two ankles from slips on ice over the past ten years, I've shifted to snowshoeing, which, like skiing, was awkward at the beginning. But now, rather than whizzing by them, I'm meeting other folks who are also out noticing the winter wildlife among the trees. It's a nice way to get a little cold-weather exercise—and for a lot less expense than skiing. I'm still happy to sit by a fire after an hour out in the cold, and I get a workout that's much more fun than my usual half hour on the treadmill at the gym.

But the real opportunity to exercise my moxie came with my early midlife crisis. I was only thirty-seven when my husband died of metastatic colorectal cancer. I'd been his caretaker intermittently for three years as he recovered first from surgery and then from chemotherapy and radiation treatments. He died three years to the day after the initial surgery that had left him with a colostomy bag and a changed attitude toward life. Not having a good prognosis, he felt that every day was to be lived to its fullest—which may have seemed selfish to others because he (and we) no longer spent our time on "shoulds" but only on "wants." That's not to say we didn't have our rough moments, when tempers flared and sadness overwhelmed, especially when he realized that he wouldn't see his children grow up. Dying puts things into perspective, that's for sure. His death and the way he approached it have had a long-term effect on my life—allowing me to encourage my moxie, if you will.

Being widowed and raising two kids, ages nine and six, was quite the challenge, I can tell you. My own resilience and help from friends made it possible to keep going.

I found a job: I had been self-employed with my own business manufacturing children's clothes, but in my changed circumstances I was unwilling to devote the time and resources to make the business grow. I went back to school part-time, kept the household running (pizza and mac and cheese notwithstanding), and made sure two kids didn't get into serious trouble. I sacrificed a social life, but it seemed a small price. We all survived, with a dose of self-confidence for each of us as a side benefit.

I got "downsized" for the first time at age forty-three and again at forty-seven. With two teenagers and their friends alone in the house after school, I suspected it was only a matter of time before some calamity occurred. So I decided once again to become my own boss and work from home, this time as a career adviser. After all, I'd had so many career directions by then that I could certainly help others with their choices. I also had the training from working as a college co-op adviser, helping over a hundred students each year to write résumés, research companies for their internships, and prep for interviewing. I was confident I could hang out my shingle as a career counselor and use those same skills to help others. And I have—for over twenty years now. I wrote the book, *Now What Do I Do? The Woman's Guide to a New Career*, published by Capital Books in 2005, to address the issues surrounding midlife career change. Now I'm writing for baby boomers like me who've arrived at the next stage (in the broadest sense) of career development—life.

Now my kids are grown and have lives of their own. At sixty-three, I took a break from my career counseling work, sold my house in Boston, where I'd lived for thirty-seven years (you can imagine the downsizing project that was!), and bought a small ranch-style house in western Massachusetts. My plan had been to find a small condo around Boston where my friends and social life were centered. But there was nothing in my price range that met my wants. I would have had to move to the exurbs about fifty minutes from where I wanted to be. I realized that if I were that far away I probably wouldn't be willing to drive back to Boston for my usual activities—meeting friends for meals, visiting museums, shopping, "game nights," or attending meetings of the various organizations I'd been part of. That got me thinking about moving even farther away. Whether I was one hour from Boston or two, I'd be starting over. But one hour away was still practically Boston, while two hours away put me into a less expensive real estate market, a rural setting, and a college town—all positives in my book. So, even though I didn't know anyone in the area, I started looking there as I was getting my house ready to sell.

None of this would have been possible without a firm understanding of my finances. I consulted a fee-only financial planner who was able to design a workable plan and set the wheels in motion for the move. It's been five years and the financial issues still make me a little nervous. I've put myself on a strict budget and have strayed only occasionally. The continuing uncertainty of the larger economy worries me, but I can only control my small piece of it. That's what I'm doing—and I hope I don't run out of resources before I run out of life! I've taken a very conservative path and continue to remain vigilant. But I'm also continuing to live the life I want, knowing that I can create a "Plan B" if things don't work out as I've envisioned. And that reflects moxie as much as making the change in the first place.

"You're so brave." "I'm jealous." These are the comments I get when I tell my story to old friends and the new people I meet. "Brave" from the folks who think they can't make radical change, not realizing sometimes that change comes anyway, whether we want it or not—the 2008 financial meltdown is a good example. I feel much more confident in decisions where I have some say, which I believe is true for most people. But I can also see their point about leaving what you know and starting over. This must be what the pioneers experienced as they headed west from the settled cities into untamed territory. At least I don't have to grow my own food or worry about the horses and wagon!

There's something refreshing in the chance to start over. Not knowing anyone nearby allows you to become the person you've wanted to be—your history will be only what you choose to share. It's a little like the witness protection program, but you get to stay in contact with family and friends (and there's no risk if your cover gets blown!).

This is the journey I'm on. Yours will be different. The important thing to recognize is that if you're unhappy with your life circumstances, other choices are possible. Remember: by not changing, you've still made a choice. You can choose to make other choices as well. Let me cheer you on as you take the steps to "mature with moxie!"

RESILIENCE

Adapting to adversity, trauma, tragedy, and stress—including family problems, moving, losing a job—is the basis of resilience. This is an ordinary response and can be learned. It doesn't mean you don't experience difficulty or distress, but rather that you have learned thoughts and actions which allow you to move on.

Developing resilience is a personal experience. According to the American Psychological Association, common factors include:

making connections with family and friends and accepting their support

interpreting highly stressful events as current crises that can be better in the future

accepting that change is part of living

moving toward personal, realistic goals by regular, small steps

taking action, rather than hoping the problem will go away

looking for opportunities to learn something about yourself

developing confidence in your problem-solving abilities

keeping things in perspective and staying positive and hopeful with an optimistic outlook

being flexible and maintaining balance whenever possible

taking care of yourself

Learn from your past. See what you have already accomplished in relation to stressful events in your life. What was helpful? Whom did you reach out to? What did you learn about yourself?

When you need help, check out support groups, self-help books, and online resources for information. If these aren't enough, help from a mental health professional may be an option.

If you don't feel confident with your current level of resiliency, begin now to expand your capacity so you're ready when "life happens."

www.apa.org/helpcenter/road-residence.aspx

2 WHO ARE YOU?

You could never plan your life in a million years.
—Judith Viorst, *Publishers Weekly*, Dec. 8, 1997

In many ways, the years after sixty resemble the teenage years: redefining who we are and what we will do, creating new relationships with family and friends, acknowledging physical changes. It's a time of uncertainty and change. The task becomes one of integrating the outer and inner worlds, defining who we are beyond our roles, work, personal history, and associations. It's a time for providing guidance and sharing wisdom. It's also a time for reflection and seeking deeper self-understanding.

What do you see when you look in the mirror? Gray hair? Wrinkles? A smile? The *you* looking back reflects many changes in your life. And there may be other changes that aren't visible in the mirror. Among them are losses, some big, some small. We probably can't run as fast, or hear or see as well, as we once did. We may have lost friends, family members, or spouses. We discover our kids are grown; we may no longer be working full-time, and there are still twenty to thirty years ahead of us. We don't have any role models to show us the way to old age. We may have saved some money and put a plan in place on how to spend it, but we usually don't have plans for what we want to do in our extended age. Our lives are not like those of our parents, so we can't use them as models for how to grow old in our time.

If we had goals in our youth, they were probably for what we would do, not who we would become. In our sixties and beyond, it's time to look at who we are, not what we do. The first half of life was involved with acquisition: relationships, property, social status, job titles, money, spouse, and children. In the second half of life it's time to relinquish the outer self and look inward. Letting go of the "shoulds" and the "oughts" allows us freedom from the past. We no longer have to be good at anything, which gives us permission to try new things and be beginners again. We may have new measures of success, which can include wisdom, well-being, and delight in the world around us, which we now have time to observe. This can be a challenging and exciting time. For some there may be an effort to regain lost youth by looking back at a time when we were happy or carefree, rather than burdened with the struggles of life. For others, it's an opportunity to make new discoveries and continue our growth and development. Or it might be a combination of these, some days focusing on the carefree and other days on moving forward.

Growing older is nothing you can fight or control. It may be possible to slow it down temporarily or disguise it, but it's impossible to stop. Finding pleasure in the process, reawakening a sense of play, and seeing things in a new light allows you to become aware of the many possibilities ahead. Knowing that time is limited leaves no room for nonsense. It's time to eliminate the unnecessary—clothes, friends who don't support you, a job that's not fulfilling, maybe even a partner.

Conducting a life review is a good place to begin. It allows you to look at your past and think about your successes and disappointments. Here are some questions to get you started:

How did you envision your life as a girl? As a teen? As a young adult? How is that different from what happened and how is it the same?

Are there past events that you're still stuck regretting? Do these disappointments and sorrows keep you from moving on?

Did you make mistakes that can still be changed?

Can you improve the relationships with your partner, your parents, your children, or your friends?

Have you talked about and shared photos of your childhood with your children and grandchildren?

If you're still working, are you happy in your job?

Are you spending time in a fulfilling way?

How's your health? Are you burned out?

Is your social life what you want?

Do you have someone you can rely on in a crisis or emergency?

Do you take time for yourself every week?

In order to move forward in life, you need to acknowledge the things that will always be part of it. Acknowledge your regrets and forgive yourself, to clear space for new relationships and interests. Recognize in yourself your resistance to change as well as your willingness to grow. It's possible to do both at the same time, or at least from day to day, depending on how you feel. If you have worries about money, are lonely, or lack family support, it's possible you might want to make changes but may not have the resources you need to do so. This may lead to resignation or depression when it becomes too challenging to make the efforts to create a new life. Your attitude also plays a part. If you feel positive about creating a new life using your resources and talents, you're more likely to be successful. If you feel life has cheated you of success, however you define it, if you are angry, or if you're stuck mourning the past, the challenges of changing your life may lead to depression rather than acceptance. Here are some ways to recognize whether you're experiencing resistance or growth.

RESISTANCE	GROWTH
Prefer the "good old days"	Are curious about today and tomorrow
Fight change	Are eager to discover self
Are unwilling to examine past	Challenge old patterns, behaviors, and communications
Find excuses not to grow: pain, physical limitations, being "set in my ways"	Adapt to loss

Chronic pain and other limitations can be barriers to change, but a realistic attitude about what's possible can lead to positive aging rather than complaining and being stuck. Everyone is different, and you need to write your own script for the next phase of your life. It begins with self-awareness and making small changes.

The journey to understand who you are often begins after a negative or traumatic event such as an illness, a divorce, the death of a good friend—really anything that has you asking what life is all about. This is often called a crisis of spirit, a time to find meaning in your life. Wealth, education, ethnicity, race, occupation, and all other demographic descriptors do not protect you from asking the question. It brings up fears of the unknown, fears about the future. While every life journey is personal, aging gives us all the opportunity to travel the path, so you're in good company.

It takes resilience to navigate the transitions of life, and a willingness to face the challenges as well as acknowledge our accomplishments. It's not possible to begin without an end. Losses are part of life—like rain. Losses include not only death, but leaving or being left. Changing, letting go, and moving on can also be losses. Lost dreams, unmet expectations, and illusions of safety and power qualify as losses as well. Your lost younger self—unwrinkled, immortal, invulnerable—counts as well. Not all losses are painful or tumultuous, like sending children off on their own. But it is only through loss that we become fully developed. You may be a drifter or a doer when tested by catastrophe. Not everyone rises to the occasion. But everyone has the potential to make changes and start again.

At sixty, parts of life are over, but others are just beginning as we move from getting ahead to getting whole. And part of that wholeness is recognizing your spiritual self, finding your soul. According to James Hollis, PhD, in *Finding Meaning in the Second Half of Life*, "Soul is the word we use to refer to the deepest intuitive relationship we have had with ourselves . . . our longing for meaning . . . and drives us toward more conscious engagement with nature and relationships with others . . . Soul is what makes us human." As we age, we're more aware of trying to answer the big questions: Who am I? Why am I here? What have I accomplished? What is the best way to live? What is the meaning of life? These are spiritual questions arising from our inner selves, our souls. You may have a religious spirituality, defined as a relationship with a higher power and observed in organized religious community services. Or you may experience an existential spirituality that is not connected to a set of widely accepted ideals or a place of worship but instead is a perspective in which you see purpose in your life and come to understand that life has an ultimate meaning and value. Spirituality is anchored by a belief system, a set of rituals, or a philosophy that speaks to your soul—what you use to make sense of what life has given you and how you help make the world a better place. If you're not in touch with your spiritual self, here are some ways to connect:

walking	meditating	journaling
cooking	exercising	creating art

Basically, you need time to yourself, time to be silent and aware. Choose something you like and can look forward to. And practice this daily, not just when you have time. You may want to create a special place where you can get comfortable with silence. You can ask questions of your inner self, or just wait to see what appears in your thoughts. A focus on gratitude, compassion, and love can get you started if you're unfamiliar with being quiet with your inner thoughts.

Your journey may return you to a place of worship, if you've left, to find other seekers. Or you may go into therapy or start a study group. We often have a glimpse of that higher something during "peak experiences" like near-death events, recreational drug use, and creating or appreciating art. You will know these experiences by the awe that you feel.

All transitions start with an ending and go in cycles or spirals, moving forward and back and forward again. Endings involve a sense of loss and sadness with letting go—of friends, places, a sense of who we were: confident, good at something. Then there is a period of emptiness, a void that is uncomfortable, and we often rush to fill it quickly. But sitting with the emptiness often helps to show the direction to move forward. Finally, there is a period of reinvention—trying new things, correcting errors of the past, deciding what is best for the next stage of the journey. Since life is a different experience for each of us, don't compare yourself and your stories with others. Be yourself and start where you are. The hardest step is to begin, but you'll emerge with new points of view and the knowledge and wisdom to continue.

Starting over means relearning a sense of yourself: what you like, what gives you satisfaction and joy, what to avoid. You'll need to attend to your spiritual needs, your emotions, your talents, and your relationships to make them what you want. You'll rebuild your life, not fix it. As with playing a computer game, when you make a mistake at level 10, you go back to the beginning. Life after sixty is a chance for another beginning. Be patient with the changes you want to make and pamper yourself to protect yourself from experiences that open old wounds. In the midst of stress, focus on where you are, what's next, and how to get there. You can still make progress with little steps. Have faith in yourself; your soul knows what you need. Just listen to it.

Of course, there may be benefits to staying stuck and not wanting to start over. Complaining, self-pity, and depression can all bring you attention and sometimes support. It takes courage to change. And it may well be worth the effort. Change is a process, as when a caterpillar turns into a butterfly—there are many stages and none can be skipped to get to the end result. And none happen overnight, either. The best antidote to complacency is to take action, no matter how small. The first step may be deciding to change.

Once on the journey to reinvention, be sure to keep an open mind about possibilities. Stay curious and listen to your inner voice. What energizes you? What drains you? Which doors are closing and which are opening? Laugh at yourself, the world, life, and death—don't take things too seriously. Feel connected to everything on earth—others, nature, thoughts, feelings—to help you contemplate who you are and how you relate to the world, your purpose. Try new things; then, depending on how you feel, keep at them or try something else instead. Start where you are and take a step in a new direction. Adapt as you go.

Action is the enemy of fear and creates new energy and courage. If you don't act, that doesn't mean there's no change. Everything changes around you, even if you're stuck and not moving. Taking charge of your own life means you can feel stuck, but you won't stay stuck. If you trust your gut, your soul, you'll know what works for you, what matters, what you want to happen. And then serendipity has a chance. When you're on your way and are open to whatever happens, you'll often be rewarded for taking action.

There is no one right way to move ahead. Act, then reflect, then repeat. Your confidence will grow, and your purpose will become clearer. You'll start to see possibilities, not problems.

You might want to acknowledge the changes in your inner life with changes on the outside to show the world that you're in the process of reinvention. Maybe that means a new hair style or lipstick color. Maybe it means a new sense of confidence in the way you get around. Or just a smile and lots of thank-yous for the little things in life. Be open and generous with your time and talents. Listen more. It doesn't take much to express the new you if it's coming from your innermost self, your soul. Who will you become?

I hope that the following chapters will help you on your journey to reinvention. Take what you find useful and leave the rest. You may want to come back to certain chapters when they apply to a particular stage in your process of change. There can be many steps to reinvention, with some changes easier than others. Try to enjoy the process.

MINI SELF-ASSESSMENT

Am I using my best talents and creativity on interesting projects?

Am I learning something new?

Am I making the world better?

Do I do something special for myself every day?

Am I sharing my expertise in a constructive way?

Do I keep an open mind about possibilities and remain curious?

Am I a good friend?

Are my relationships healthy?

Do I have a sense of purpose and look for life's meaning?

Do I laugh enough?

3 WORKING 9 TO 5?

I think the girl who is able to earn her own living and pay her own way should be as happy as anybody on earth.
—Susan B. Anthony, quoted in Ida Husted Harper's
The Life and Work of Susan B. Anthony

Work means different things to different people. While for some work is a chore, an unpleasant necessity that they'd rather not have to face, and which they'd give up at the first reasonable opportunity, for many of us work is something that delivers far more than a paycheck. It's a reason to get up in the morning, a way to feel that our time is being used productively. Work gives our lives meaning and drives us forward.

Do you want or need to work for a paycheck? If the answer is yes, you can then decide if you'll work for someone else or work for yourself. But before you get into the nitty-gritty of looking for a position, it's important to (1) know what you bring to the party, and (2) figure out what you want to do.

If you're going to continue with the work that you've already been doing, maybe with some modifications such as a shorter workweek or less travel, then you just need to work out the details. That should be fairly easy. On the other hand, if you're going to make a career change because you've relocated, you've been downsized, or you're simply ready for a change, then the process is more involved.

While it can be a challenge to look for work at any age, after sixty it can be even more of a project. Age discrimination is alive and well in most workplaces. The human resources staff and hiring managers are young enough to be your children (or grandchildren), and they unconsciously view you as they do their relatives. Usually this does not include a high regard for your computer and technical skills or other specific abilities required for the job.

It's important that you anticipate a negative response when you submit a résumé, and especially when you interview. To help overcome the ageism bias, be sure to emphasize your up-to-date computer and Internet skills (and if these skills aren't current, then get some training so they are). Next, emphasize how you've successfully worked with people across the age spectrum. You need to be seen as willing and able to take direction rather than being the authority or an "I know better" employee.

Finally, be sure to exhibit energy and enthusiasm. This means action verbs on your résumé—which should only include employment for the past ten years. When you show up for the interview, shatter the stereotypes. Make sure that your hair, accessories, and dress are not dowdy. Greet everyone involved in the interview with a warm smile, walk briskly across the room to shake hands, and sit at the front of your chair. All of these things will convey energy.

Once you've decided to look for work, taking the next step can be easy. Jobs can be found anywhere and everywhere—you just need to look for them. Here are a few stories illustrating some of the possibilities for new job directions taken by "just folks." If they can make these changes, so can you! Your imagination is the limit, but serendipity may play a role, too. Jumping at an opportunity when it presents itself can make all the difference. That's just what happened to Andrea.

Andrea had already made a radical midcareer move to become a lawyer at age fifty-eight after a career as a high school history teacher. But after law school graduation, litigating in the New York

District Attorney's office for four years was only one of her careers. She also went on to be the assistant dean of students at her alma mater, and later left that position to go back to teaching—in Amman, Jordan.

King's Academy was established to give bright but poor students from across Jordan the opportunity to pursue an advanced education. This boarding school is a locus for international studies and many of the classes are conducted in English. Jordan's king had attended boarding school in the United States as a teen and wanted to create a similar experience for students at King's Academy. The headmaster knew Andrea from her teaching days and thought she might be willing to sign on as part of the original faculty. She would be designing programs and curriculum as well as teaching in the classroom. Without hesitation, she packed her bags and headed to the Middle East.

She admits she was ill prepared for her role as the sole female faculty member, which led her to become the de facto counselor for all female students. Discussions in her classrooms had to be structured so that various political and religious opinions could be voiced in a neutral atmosphere. And the girls were required to speak in class, not something they had previously been encouraged to do. In addition to seeing her students in class, Andrea was invited to many of their homes, often riding on a bus for hours through the desert, alongside passengers and a driver who spoke no English.

Her years in Amman included tragedies along with triumphs, as lives everywhere do. But living on the other side of the globe in a non-Western culture was worth the sunburn, stomach upsets, and bouts of loneliness. However, when her contract came up for renewal, she declined. After three years she saw the first co-ed class graduate, then headed home with photos and memories she's now compiling into a memoir. She stays in contact with many of her students via Facebook. Most are now college grads from schools across Europe, Asia, and the United States. Her newest project is working with a school for girls in Afghanistan, mentoring students and faculty via Skype.

Like Andrea, you may do something you've done before, but in a new way. Your job change may not be as radical as Andrea's, but why not look beyond the usual opportunities? Like any job, your next one doesn't have to last forever. Here's what one couple did.

Art was vice president of human resources for a regional bank when it was bought by a larger bank conglomerate and he was let go. He fully expected to find a new position before his small severance package expired. But when six months turned into nearly a year, Art realized he might not find a comparable job. At sixty-two, it was quite possible he might not find another job, period. When his wife, Joanne, lost her position as a marketing manager when her employer relocated out of state, they felt desperate. But once the panic subsided, they realized they now had the opportunity to do something they'd thought about for retirement: buy a small camper and visit all the national parks.

Their children thought they were crazy, but with some planning and a home equity loan, it became possible. They arranged to rent their house and headed west. With no specific timetable and only each other for company, there were some bleak days after the initial excitement wore off. They adjusted their itinerary, adding specific dates and destinations rather than just pointing themselves toward the next park. That structure helped give the trip more meaning, as did their decision to check out job prospects in cities and towns they found appealing. At campgrounds along the way, they chatted with other older couples, most of whom had retired and were full of advice about what to see, but not much help when it came to job openings. However, at Yosemite they struck gold, although at the time they didn't realize it.

Camping next to Art and Joanne one night was a couple who had been employed as caretakers for a senior community near Phoenix. They were on their way to a new assignment in Sacramento and had decided to take a few days of vacation before settling in. The company they worked for had several facilities, and it was often looking for couples to manage them. As Art and Joanne headed north on the road to Crater Lake, they talked at length about the possibility of becoming managers of a 55+ community. At the next town they used the Internet at the public library to research the business's operations, then called the corporate headquarters in Las Vegas and made an appointment to learn more. Since both of them had already been looking for jobs, their résumés were up-to-date on their laptop, so they printed copies, ready to take to the interview. Instead of going north, they headed east, with Las Vegas now their next destination.

Today, Art and Joanne manage a senior community in San Diego and take their five-year-old camper to Palm Springs, Death Valley, and into Baja for weekend jaunts when the respite managers are on-site. They still rent out their house near Chicago, but are thinking about selling it, since they don't imagine they'll be moving back. The kids now believe this was a great job choice—one none of them would have thought of. And the kids credit their parents with having more gumption than they believed. For now, it's a great career choice for both Art and Joanne.

Art and Joanne were open and willing to try something new. Maybe you want to look for a job in a new field, the way Pam did.

Pam worked for a national nonprofit that had decided to consolidate offices—her New England branch was going to be merged with the New York City office. She was given eighteen months' notice and offered a position in New York, but at sixty-three she didn't want to leave family and friends in Boston.

With a work history in marketing and advertising in the for-profit sector, she had taken the job with this nonprofit when her previous firm was taken over. She'd enjoyed the change to the nonprofit world, believing she was making a difference. For many years she'd been a volunteer for the Jimmy Fund, first helping with logistics and then as a cyclist in the annual Pan-Mass Challenge fundraiser. Those experiences led her to look to the nonprofit world when she'd needed a new job.

Pam had not been prepared for the significant salary cut, however. She had rationalized with herself that the lower-stress working environment among friendly co-workers would be worth the switch. But, as in any organization with lots of moving parts, the interpersonal relationships had their tensions, and Pam's stress levels went up and down with deadlines and budget cuts. When the consolidation was announced, Pam was actually relieved and ready to move on to something else.

But six years after her last job search, she felt that her age was working against her. She searched online, used her LinkedIn network to find and apply for jobs, and told all her friends and colleagues she was looking for a new position. Four months and at least ten interviews later, she finally was offered a job at an even lower salary than when she'd first moved to the nonprofit world. Worried that she wouldn't get another offer, she accepted and began her job as a communications assistant, still another downshift from her previous job responsibilities. Two months into the job she felt completely out of place—she was the oldest employee other than the director. Her colleagues spent a fair amount of time socializing outside the workplace, and while they were not unkind to Pam, she felt ignored when it came to office chit-chat and being a part of group projects.

Lunch with a friend started the wheels in motion for another job change, when their discussion of old times and past plans reminded Pam that this job wasn't where she really wanted to be. Seven months after starting, Pam left for another nonprofit that fits her needs better: one with an older work group, some travel, and a better salary. There's a downside—an hour-long commute—but she's hoping she'll be able to work from home once she's become familiar with the scope of her job. She also hopes this job will last at least until she can retire with full Social Security and Medicare benefits.

If your new job doesn't fit, like Pam's, be willing to try again. Of course, maybe you've always had a dream of being your own boss. What would it take to make that dream a reality? Here's Debbie's story.

Debbie left her anesthesiology group at age sixty-three, a little young to retire for many in medicine, but she felt that the exorbitant malpractice insurance rates she had to pay weren't justified in her small New Hampshire hospital. She chose to become a full-time farmer instead.

She was a city girl, having grown up in Cleveland, then studying and practicing medicine in New York and Boston before making the midlife move to set up practice in New Hampshire. There was nothing in her experience that would indicate agrarian dreams.

Closing up shop was easier than she'd expected. A young doctor was eager to take over her practice, and within three months of making her decision, Debbie was jobless. Since New Hampshire's best field crop is boulders, she decided on raising animals. But which ones were the best choice? How many should she keep? What facilities would she need to build, or, more likely, have built?

She started with two goats and a dozen chickens. The billy goat had to be traded after only six months because he kept breaking

out of the fenced area and charging anyone who approached—
even Debbie, who got knocked to the ground one time too many.
The new nanny she traded him for came with a kid, giving her a
"herd" of three. Debbie soon learned that foxes can spook goats,
not just chickens. A closed structure, not quite a barn, was the
next addition, so that the goats could be inside at night, rather
than huddled under the lean-to. There was plenty of extra room in
the new shelter, so next came the six sheep and finally, two years
later, the llama.

Of course, during this time Debbie started hanging out at the
feed supply store, which was where she learned about the New
England Small Farm Institute. She met folks who were seasoned
hands as well as other newbies like herself. After a time, she met
a sheep shearer who agreed to visit her farm in the spring, and
cheese makers who would come to the farm for milk when the kids
and lambs were weaning. She also found a butcher to take the extra
lambs and chickens.

The only missing ingredient, as any farmer will tell you, is vacation time. Debbie's partner, Marie, has put her foot down and
demands that she find a manager for the farm, at least part-time,
so they can visit the Grand Canyon and other places on their bucket
list.

To see Debbie in her overalls and plaid shirt you'd never guess
she'd once been a highly paid medical specialist in Boston. She
claims that's the work that gave her all her gray hair.

This may be the time to change career direction to something
you've always wanted to do. Not interested in the farming lifestyle? Maybe Mary's business choice will give you some ideas.

Mary took the plunge to start her own business. As often happens,
job change was thrust on Mary rather than being her choice. As a

dietitian, Mary had worked for the Special Supplemental Nutrition Program for Women, Infants, and Children, better known as WIC, in Virginia, but in late 2006 the grant she worked under was not renewed and funding for her project ran out. Part of her job included developing software to monitor and educate clients, a skill she decided she could apply to her own business.

Instead of looking for a new job as a dietitian, she toyed with the idea of starting her own travel business. She loved going to Ireland, where she had stayed with distant family members and even in convents around the country . She had also organized an extended family reunion in Texas, making all of the plane, hotel, and car rental arrangements for the forty-seven people who attended. Without a job, the prospect of creating destination travel packages to Ireland, and from Ireland to New York and Boston, was moved to the front burner. She devoted a year to learn about the travel industry and make connections with vendors.

It's possible to create a virtual business online with low overhead and minimal start-up costs. In October 2007 Mary launched her online travel business. Then came the 2008 financial collapse. She sublet her apartment and moved in with her sister's family to make ends meet as she persisted with the travel business. To keep her accounts active with the airlines she offered to book flights for friends. She organized a cruise on the St. Lawrence Seaway for an Iowa family's reunion. And she got herself a job at the local Starbucks, so that she'd have health insurance coverage and a small income to help pay for groceries.

Fast forward to today. Mary now organizes special "fiber" trips, which include all the arrangements for a cruise or overland trip, accompanied by a well-known knitter, crocheter, or quilter. She works with yarn and quilt shops along the route. The expert presents a talk or workshop for the locals as well as the trip participants, and shop owners offer specials on their wares. Past events have included a cruise to Bermuda for crochet enthusiasts with an Australian crochet teacher, sheep-to-wool trips in England and the United States, and a creative fiber cruise to Alaska. She's also partnered with another small travel business, which she found online, to promote destination bar and bat mitzvahs.

Mary's made a business in a "dead" industry by finding a niche that works. She's been successful enough that she's just purchased a little Irish cottage where she spends as much time as possible and plans to retire—someday.

Mary's success was possible because she did something else while developing her business.

What's your dream job? Starting a used bookstore? Becoming an actor? Running a bed and breakfast? Now may be just the time to start your own business. Just don't risk everything! Information about starting a business can be found in the Resources section of this book.

Whether you're self-employed or working for someone else, it's important to remember that all good jobs have one thing in common—they match the interests, skills, values, and work style of each individual. Taking the time to identify the right job, the one that best matches your unique abilities and interests, will result in a more satisfying choice and offer additional direction on where and what to look for. You may already have some ideas.

If you can describe your ideal job, you're more likely to find one that meets your needs. Think about what kind of work you'd like to do, where you'd like to do it, and with whom. Once you've discovered your ideal job, it's possible to translate it into a practical equivalent. Taking a little time to imagine your perfect job is an investment toward finding the best available option.

Assume you've been given a million dollars, no strings (or taxes) attached. What would you do more of? What would you do less of? Or, pretend you're ninety-five and looking back. What do you want to remember about your work and, more important, yourself?

Just close your eyes and envision your new workplace. What does the space look like? Is it indoors or out? Who are you working with? How do you get to work? What are you wearing? What are you earning? And of course, What are you doing? Repeat this exercise over several days, with your eyes closed, and see how your vision changes. Just remember, this is *your ideal job*, not anyone else's ideas for you. When you feel your vision is complete, jot down your thoughts. This can become the blueprint as you look for a job or plan your own business. The closer your "real job" is to your ideal, the happier you'll be.

Here's an example of an ideal job description. Yours will be quite different, but notice the detail. The more you know about what you want, the easier it is to determine the non-negotiable aspects as you look for something new.

I work for a consulting company that specializes in environmental issues. There are several small offices in various cities. Each office employs about five to seven people, including three or four consultants who work as a team (lawyer, economist, ecologist, public policy analyst) with assistants and student interns. Each office works primarily on local and regional environmental questions for government and industry officials. Other environmental agencies are the competition.

I am one of the consultants (public policy analyst) in the Dallas office. Each team member works independently and is responsible to other team members. A loosely connected relationship exists with the other offices for sharing information.

As the policy analyst, it's my responsibility to synthesize the information provided by the other team members and create reports of the findings to present to the legislature, industry leaders, and the public. I also "schmooze" with government leaders at the state and local levels. I feel successful when the project is completed, has been presented, and is acted upon. I need to be articulate, good at talking on my feet, a good writer, and a good negotiator, so that I can get all the information I need. The future is bright, since much government agency work of this kind is being privatized.

My work schedule is somewhat erratic, as I need to spend some evenings making public presentations. For the most part I can arrange my own hours. Sometimes the workload is light, at other times—close to deadlines—heavy, but I work an average of twenty to thirty hours per week. Travel is local for the most part and does not interfere too much with nonworking time. Because my schedule is somewhat flexible, I can arrange both my working and nonworking time to meet my needs.

My pay is around $75,000 and will rise to $90,000 within two years. This amount is all salary. I contribute to a company 401(k) retirement plan, as well as my own IRA. Health benefits are available at a competitive price, which I buy as a group member.

Now it's your turn!

Once you have your ideal job figured out, it's time to examine the details of your interests, skills, values, and work style to find a job or a business that will not only meet your needs, but also make you want to jump out of bed each morning to get to work.

We'll start with interests. Think about all your past jobs—paid and unpaid. What did you like? Be specific here: "Work with people" is not a good answer. Did you mean "caring for young children" or "being on a product development team?" Or maybe it was "counseling others," or "teaching." Do you see why specifics are important? The point is for you to discover the core tasks, the things you can transfer from one job to another, whether in the same or a different field. Start by making a list of tasks you performed in your past jobs. Add any hobbies you cultivate, leisure

activities, family activities, and other activities that you participate in. What do you really enjoy doing? What do you still want
to do? Brainstorm with others if you like. Be descriptive. Think in
terms of job tasks rather than job titles. It's important to find the
kind of work you want to do, no matter what it's called. This is
your list—make it as long as you like.

Once you have an idea of your interests and can describe your
ideal job, the next step is to shift the focus to your skills. It's important to recognize that you have skills that might not have been
used on the job. You'll need to be honest as you look at yourself
and what you can do. Don't over- or undervalue your abilities.

Again, make a comprehensive list of everything you can do,
even if you don't like to do it—you'll narrow this list down later.
Try to get two hundred items on your list—it's easier than you
think if you include everything: supervise others (employees,
children, housekeeper), write reports, drive safely, repair broken
lamps, organize projects, manage a budget, invent things, get
along with people, and so on. The items will keep adding up. Add
in the things you *know*. Think about all the things you've learned,
either on the job or through formal schooling or training—insurance sales techniques, Internet research, knowing zoning bylaws,
and any other category of knowledge. Your list will reach two hundred items before you know it.

Once you have your list, identify about fifteen items you want
to do frequently (several times each week), about fifteen items
you want to do often (several times a month), and about ten items
you'll be happy doing occasionally (once per month or less). Don't
feel obliged to include tasks that you don't really want to do; although "filing" is on my long list, it won't make it to any of the
shorter ones!

Now look at these shorter lists and see if the items fall into
categories or show a clear relationship to one another, such as

"communication," "helping others," or "creativity." These are the skills you should seek to use as part of your next work experience. The focus now shifts to values, the inner guide that's a critical part of job satisfaction. It's usually a clash of values that makes us change jobs—or that gets us fired! It's our gut reactions to activities and people that make many jobs difficult to stay with over prolonged periods of time. If you don't agree with the company's actions, you'll start behaving in ways that will get you a pink slip. It's sometimes unconscious, but always a reflection of who you are and what you believe. That's why having a values match is extremely important for job satisfaction.

As you think about what's important to you now, you probably are not interested in what motivated you in your early- and mid-career phases. It's unlikely that your goals have remained static, so if your job hasn't changed with you, this may be the impetus to make changes now. At this stage in your life and career, one thing is probably truer now than ever—you're unwilling to compromise your values for the job.

To get started, think about what the following terms mean to you. Don't try to regurgitate a dictionary definition. Instead give your own personal interpretation. How you interpret these terms determines how meaningful each is to you.

Write down your meanings for each and then select six that are most relevant to you today. These are the items to discuss in

Friends	Spirituality	Family
Leisure	Health and fitness	Community service
Content of work	Spouse/Partner	Contribution to society
Security	Co-workers	Geographical location
Influence and power	Income	Workplace environment

relation to your new job. The closer the fit, the better you'll like the work. Just remember that new issues may come along to unexpectedly change your priorities. If a family member gets ill and you need to care for that person, for example, that becomes your first priority, even if it wasn't one of the six on your list. For now, in your current circumstances, the six you choose are the most important.

Finally, what's your temperament? How do you approach life? Are you easygoing or do you prefer schedules? Do you like working alone or with others? When job demands are a close match to your preferences, you'll find greater satisfaction in the work you're doing. Trouble is waiting to happen if there's a mismatch of your values and temperament with the job's expectations. Save yourself the stress by knowing who you are and how you work best and using that knowledge to your advantage.

Once you've completed your job search profile—interests, skills, values, and temperament—it's time to think about whether you'll work for yourself or for someone else, for pay or as a volunteer. Or maybe you'll decide not to work at all! Oh, the possibilities! There are many job search and business start-up guides in the Resources section.

IF YOU DON'T NEED FULL-TIME EMPLOYMENT

There are many options for earning outside a full-time job. Here are some possibilities:

music / art / hobbies: sales at craft shows or online (iTunes, Etsy)

temping: possibly leading to full-time work, or not
(H&R Block, Kelly Temps)

teaching: share what you know (Road Scholar, adult-ed programs, shelters, nursing homes)

virtual assistant / guru: from any location, help others
(Fiverr, Upwork)

4 RANDOM ACTS OF KINDNESS

You will do something outside yourself, something to repair tears in your community, something to make life a little better for people less fortunate than you. That's what I think a meaningful life is — one lives not just for oneself, but for one's community.
—Ruth Bader Ginsburg, Stanford University Rathbun Lecture, 2017

Should you be a volunteer? After accumulating a lifetime of experience, you can offer much as a volunteer. Your time and talents will be greatly appreciated by both the organization you contribute to and, with luck, your own psyche. There are so many underfunded and understaffed nonprofits out there that finding the one that's the best fit for your skills and interests might be the bigger challenge.

Volunteers stuff envelopes, tutor children, counsel people in crisis, sell tickets, and act as guides, as well as serve on the boards that govern these organizations. There are opportunities for local, state, national, and international participation. Here are a few stories about the volunteer contributions made by regular people like you and me. Cyndi's experience brought her adventure as well as great satisfaction.

Cyndi leaves the comfort of her St. Louis suburb for six weeks each year, three in April and three in October. This is her tenth year participating as a nurse with the St. Brigid's Catholic Church Haiti service project. The enthusiastic reports she shares each time she returns have made her an informal ambassador for the program.

A team of one doctor, two nurses, two medical students, and a cook operates each field clinic in rural Haiti. A field clinic doesn't look like much. One large tent for both thorough examinations and minor surgery, with a table and several chairs covered by a canopy serving as the space for assessment, education, and dispensing medication, constitutes the whole clinic. Villagers travel on foot to receive care, sometimes walking for days over rugged terrain, arriving with infected wounds, sick children, and general malnutrition. Many patients have left others behind who are too ill or injured to travel. When possible, someone from the medical team visits them, but it's frequently not possible.

The first year Cyndi had been overwhelmed by the poverty, not to mention the spartan living conditions, which required her to help dig a latrine. Flying insects were everywhere, and sleeping on a raised cot was essential to escape the slithering critters in the night. But every day she knew she was helping, in some small way at least, to make life a little better for all of the people she treated, with a simple eye salve or wound cleaning and stitches. She'd never felt so needed, even after having spent her whole career as a nurse. No matter what it was, everything she did in Haiti, even something as small as holding a child's hand during a physical exam, was appreciated.

Because of the great need, the mountain clinics were rarely set up in the same area twice. But today, with an expanded program due to both the influx of donations after the 2010 earthquake and a greater awareness of all health-related programs in Haiti, more permanent clinics have been set up, and Cyndi returns each spring to one and each fall to another. She's been doing this long enough to have seen children grow up and elders die, and now it feels as if she's lost a family member each time that happens. Now, at age seventy, she plans to continue raising awareness at home and spending less time in the clinics. And after six weeks in the Haitian mountains, she always greatly appreciates the luxury of having a refrigerator when she gets home.

Don't feel you want to travel to poverty-stricken countries to share your expertise and enthusiasm? Worry not! There are plenty of opportunities closer to home.

Marge was finding her days awfully long since retiring. She'd golfed, played tennis, joined a book group at the library, and met former colleagues for lunch once a month. But that wasn't enough. After she moaned to her lunch buddies about being a little bored, someone suggested she find a volunteer job. When she protested that she didn't want to stuff envelopes or shelve books, the idea of doing something at the science museum came up. Hmmm. Marge had been a pharmacist, so something in science might appeal.

She contacted the volunteer department and now has a weekly gig. As "MADam Scientist," complete with lab coat and crazy wig, she creates lightning from static electricity, generates electricity from potatoes, and turns liquids from red to blue to green in front of audiences of elementary school students on field trips. Marge's playful nature and ham acting come out on stage, making her one of the volunteers who get top ratings on the students' evaluations.

But Marge has found a way to contribute even more. She's now on the volunteer board of the science museum and has helped bring special exhibits to the museum by tapping into her business network. She even stuffs envelopes now and again.

Like the theater? Interested in politics? Just want to make new friends? There's somewhere you can use your skills, no matter what those skills are. Nonprofits depend on volunteers to succeed. You don't necessarily need experience—many jobs, even volunteer jobs, come with training. This could be your chance to try something new. That's what Bob and Betty Ann did.

Bob had served in the Air Force and then became a commercial airline pilot, which brought mandatory retirement at age sixty. What was he supposed to do with himself now? He wasn't yet a doting grandfather, and as much as he loved golf he could only play once a week or risk aggravating bursitis in his shoulder. He started teaching flight ground school classes at a Denver community college, but that lost its luster after the third semester of repetition.

Betty Ann was a homemaker and had raised four children, often alone, when Bob was flying multiday trips. An excellent seamstress, she still made costumes for the high school drama department long after their youngest child had graduated. Bob puttered in his workshop, building shelves for any available wall and birdhouses that he sold at the annual church Christmas bazaar.

Days went by without any focus, and Bob was showing the first signs of depression—lethargy and lack of interest. Betty Ann worried he would get worse and started researching volunteer activities Bob might like. Habitat for Humanity was a logical choice, since it would take advantage of Bob's building skills, which he thoroughly enjoyed putting to use. She talked him into trying his hand at the next project that was scheduled in Denver.

In short, Bob loved it and signed on for another project as soon as the first was finished. He nailed and drilled to his heart's content and learned new skills, such as installing windows and doors. Soon he was even thinking of building a small cabin for himself and Betty Ann and started searching for land in the nearby Rocky Mountains.

Once Habitat had Bob and Betty Ann's contact information, they sent materials about projects in other states, on Native American reservations, and in Central America and the Caribbean. Bob's enthusiasm for his projects was contagious, and a year after the first project began, they'd signed up to help with a Guatemalan project. Now they're Habitat regulars, making an annual pilgrimage to a project site in a Spanish-speaking country. Betty Ann had been a language major in college and her reimmersion in Spanish brought back her skills and made her a treasured member of the team.

Coupled with her ability to sew curtains and pillows, the chance to speak Spanish made her as engaged as Bob in the success of each project.

When they're not on a building site, Betty Ann and Bob sponsor fund-raising events to cover their costs (each participant pays for transportation, food, and lodging) and, with luck, enough over to make a contribution to the school or hospital near the building site. To date they've been to Guatemala and Honduras, twice to each, and are wondering where they'll go next.

Have these stories sparked your imagination to figure out what you can do? You don't necessarily have to get involved with an ongoing project or organization—you can sponsor your own, as Nancy did after her daughter was killed in a car accident on her way to work one February morning.

Katie had been a vivacious, twenty-seven-year-old second grade teacher in Indiana, much loved by her students and fellow faculty. Her enthusiasm and sunny disposition were sorely missed. Her divorced mother, Nancy, and two brothers were devastated. All three children were living at home at the time. Jon, thirty-one, had moved back to attend grad school; Brandon, thirty, had lost his job; and Katie had been saving for a down payment on a condo. The house echoed without her.

They grieved and went through the motions of getting back to normal, but normal had changed. As the first anniversary of Katie's death approached, the family wanted something special to remember her by. After a lot of brainstorming and thinking about Katie's interests, they decided to create a scholarship fund for deserving Indiana college students who wanted to become teachers. Since their own resources were not plentiful enough to do this, they sponsored a 5K run/walk race and planned it as a family event, not just something for runners. There were T-shirts for the racers, as well as prizes donated from local merchants. Balloons, popcorn, a fire engine, and donated pony rides turned the race into a broader event. They raised over $8,000 from race registrations and donations that first year, which translated into three $2,000 scholarships (with the remainder kept as seed money for the second annual event).

Nancy, now sixty-six, created and runs the small foundation that has turned the race into part of a larger effort. Since that first event they've sponsored breakfasts for families who've lost children and designed service projects to support causes Katie believed in, including homeless shelters and animal rescue groups. The foundation isn't huge, but it still awards scholarships each spring. And every May the road is closed, the popcorn popped, and the starting gun goes off for the annual tribute to Katie.

Your volunteer experience doesn't have to be exotic or extensive. Most organizations are unlikely to turn you away. Volunteering can even lead to a paid position, if you're interested. Volunteer opportunities are everywhere—as close as your computer and as distant as the far side of the world.

How do you find the volunteer opportunity that suits you best? Unfortunately, nonprofit organizations can rarely afford to publicize their volunteer openings, so finding them can be a challenge. There are several online databases that make matching volunteers and needy organizations easier. Look at www.idealist. org, www.charitynavigator.org, or www.volunteermatch.org to get started. Check your local newspaper and TV news programs. They often announce or advertise volunteer needs. Don't forget to ask around for recommendations from friends and family.

Your local *public library* can always use help, whether it's shelving books, reading to children, delivering books to shut-ins, helping to organize a book sale, or keeping the grounds neat. Just pay a visit to the head librarian and offer your services to see what tasks need doing.

If you have a grandchild in *school* (and even if you don't), why not volunteer in a classroom or after school program? Or in the school library. Or around the office. Schools always have a need for extra hands, hearts, and minds. If you haven't spent time at school since you graduated (except possibly for PTA meetings or Back-to-School nights to meet the teachers), you'll be in for an education. There's lots going on with computers, sports, field trips, and so on where you can help out. Maybe you'll learn a thing or two while you're sharing what you know. If you're interested in more of a commitment, schools sometimes welcome part-time volunteer classroom helpers, cafeteria monitors, or folks to help manage traffic at dismissal. Sometimes they even pay these people.

Have you ever wanted to be a TV or radio personality? Community access *cable television* is waiting for you! Whether in front of or behind the camera there are plenty of things to do: hold the microphone, operate a camera, create stage sets, answer phones, go on the scene for interviews, work in the control room, or even produce your own program—the list is huge. This may be your chance to break into the entertainment field. *Public television* and *radio stations* are always looking for volunteers, too—and for a lot more than just answering the phones during pledge drives.

Don't forget to check out your local *police* and *fire departments*. In this period of fiscal cutbacks these public servants are stretched to the max. Maybe they have some tasks they can turn over to you to make their jobs easier. There may be filing or other paperwork that isn't getting done as they answer increased numbers of calls for help. Or maybe they need assistance learning new computer software or distributing information across the community. Drop by to find out—and while you're there tell them what a great job they're doing.

Interested in politics? There are *cause-related organizations* for everything from running for office to helping prevent forest fires. There's something for everyone. Whether you want to help beautify the roadways, reduce drug use among teens, improve local hiking trails, or increase awareness of domestic abuse, there's a group or activity you can join. Of course, there are also religious organizations, homeless shelters, rehabilitation centers for disabled workers, reading for the blind—the list goes on and on.

Many volunteer opportunities require specific skills such as teaching, carpentry, counseling, or management. Others provide training you'll need, like CPR or homework assistance. Do something that matches your professional skills, your interests, or that you find to be just plain fun.

One of the largest volunteer organizations is the *United Way,* which acts almost like a charity for charities and can plug you in to many different organizations in your area. If you love the outdoors and helping to educate people about the nation's need for conservation, wildlife, and park history, you may well find your calling as a volunteer for the *US National Park Service.* If you are a history or science buff who has never been able to find the right forum, think about participating in reenactments, helping at archeological digs, conducting museum tours, or even tracking down an opportunity for museum management.

There are many volunteer jobs located overseas. The *Peace Corps* is the most famous overseas volunteer organization in the world. They recruit anyone with a college degree in any field to teach skills and share knowledge. The Peace Corps operates in virtually every country on earth, serving a variety of needs. And don't think that it's only for kids: older volunteers are more numerous than ever.

Whether it's in your neighborhood, or at the city, state, national, or even international level, make the effort to help in a cause you believe in. You'll meet great people while you're at it—and your efforts will make a difference in someone else's life. So how do you know if a volunteer opportunity is the right one for you? Think of finding a volunteer position in the same way that you looked for the perfect job in chapter 3. For more specific questions to ask and a more detailed way to assess your choices, see the chapter on volunteering in my book, *Now What Do I Do?* (Capital Press, 2005).

Before you volunteer, research those organizations you've found that match your interests, just as you would if you were donating your money instead of your time. Wouldn't you hate to find out that you donated your time to an organization that went bankrupt, instead of to one that was pursuing the same mission and had enough cash flow to sustain its work well into the future? Or maybe you see an opportunity to help a charity whose revenue hasn't grown as quickly as the need for its programs, and which could really use your help. Do your research to make sure you're putting your hard work toward a legitimate and financially viable organization. Unfortunately, the only data currently available for analyzing charities is financial information: how much a charity spends on fundraising and other overhead, what it pays its CEO, how large its endowment. For large organizations, you can review their annual reports on paper or online. Guidestar.org and FoundationCenter.org are two sources. For smaller organizations, it's often much more difficult. Check with local Better Business Bureaus and state oversight divisions of the attorney general's office. IRS.gov offers searches for Form 990N filed by small tax-exempt organizations. Additionally, investigate the success of an organization's programs by looking for news stories.

Once you've created a list of potential volunteer opportunities, you'll need to begin comparing them. Find out what each organization's needs are and see how they match your interests and skills. Avoid "giving it a try" and then quitting if you don't like it. Organizations depend on their volunteers and can ill afford abrupt starts and stops when volunteers just quit. Instead, meet with the volunteer manager and ask questions about the organization and its environment. Ask if you can talk with other volunteers or spend a day shadowing someone before you sign up. You should expect to be interviewed to see if your time availability and skills are a match. Be prepared for background checks, references, and possibly immunizations and tuberculosis tests. And be patient. It's important to give yourself time to explore a variety of opportunities among different agencies.

Recent years have brought a new twist on volunteering: going virtual by allowing volunteers to complete tasks online. Virtual volunteering allows agencies to expand the benefits of their programs without requiring onsite participation.

Many people actively search for virtual volunteer opportunities because they have personal reasons that don't allow them to participate onsite—maybe transportation or mobility issues, childcare responsibilities, or only intermittent time availability. Virtual volunteering allows anyone to contribute time and expertise to nonprofit organizations, schools, government offices, and other agencies that use volunteer services. Virtual volunteer opportunities can be discovered either on each nonprofit's website or through www.volunteermatch.com.

As a volunteer, you should want to donate your time and energy to an organization and a cause that you care about. You will profit immensely from your volunteer experience, whether you work once a month at a local homeless shelter or spend a year providing health care in Tanzania. You'll develop new skills, new perspectives, new contacts, and new opportunities, and if you've chosen the right position, you'll find inspiration and pleasure in what you do. If you can be flexible, productive, dependable, and a hard worker, you'll make a difference—for others and yourself!

VOLUNTEER RESPONSIBILITIES

Take your responsibilities as a volunteer seriously. If you expect to be treated professionally, you need to behave that way. Here are some guidelines:

Be supportive, loyal, and enthusiastic. Don't volunteer unless you feel passionate about the organization or the project.

Be punctual. Don't cancel five minutes before you're due to arrive, end your "year" abroad after only three months, or just forget to show up. Every time a volunteer fails to show up, it's a lost opportunity for an organization that probably already has fewer resources than it needs. To avoid this problem, analyze your schedule and come up with a realistic number of hours you can commit. You can always increase your commitment after you've volunteered for a while.

Complete the jobs you accept.

Stay informed about policies and procedures. Get the necessary training whenever possible.

When required, pay dues, attend meetings, and keep accurate records.

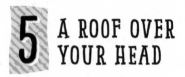

5 A ROOF OVER YOUR HEAD

There's no place like home.
There's no place like home.
There's no place like home.
—Dorothy, in Frank Baum's *The Wizard of Oz*

In talking with hundreds of older people, one of the most common questions I've heard is, "What should I do—stay or move?" Whether you're sixty or ninety, trying to figure out the right living arrangement can be a challenge. Life circumstances have often changed. You may be alone, by choice or not. You may have a spouse, partner, or other "roommates" whose needs and preferences also need to be considered. What worked when you were housing a growing family may no longer be relevant. Illness or just the "creakiness" of growing older may make mobility an important factor that it wasn't just a few years ago.

There's no single "right" answer to the question of where you should live. The information on the following pages is designed to help you think about your wants and needs. Sometimes a systematic approach to finding a solution works. But other times it's just serendipity—as happened in my case.

I knew it was time to leave the home where I'd raised my kids. They'd both relocated to California several years earlier, and it was always easier—and cheaper—for me to visit them instead of the other way around. I was rattling around alone in a house with too much space for one person, frittering away too much of my time cleaning, and spending way too much of my modest income on maintenance, taxes, and utilities. But where to go? Most of my friends were in Boston, and all the social and interest groups I belonged to were there as well: book discussion, church choir, business colleagues, and those friends I met regularly for lunch or dinner. My first thought was to downsize but stay in the area. I looked at smaller houses and condos within a ten-mile radius of my home. I wanted a community where I could walk to the post office, the library, and some shops, maybe even to a grocery store. In looking at the available properties, I realized I wanted two bedrooms, because the total living space was larger. I wanted covered parking, so that I wouldn't have to dig my car out of the inevitable and sometimes frequent snow of a New England winter. I also realized I needed to be able to have space outdoors, even if it was only a balcony barely large enough to sit and enjoy a cup of coffee. I didn't know all this at the beginning; I learned it from going to many, many open houses, so many that I sometimes forgot which property had the unlivable black-and-chartreuse bathroom, or which had twelve steps up to get into the building, then a climb up twelve more to reach the unit I was interested in.

I also learned that my budget was too small for these suburban choices, so I started looking farther out. When I reached towns where I could afford a space the size I wanted, I was an hour away from where I'd first started looking. I had to ask myself whether I would realistically drive for an hour to meet a friend for lunch. Not only the time, but the cost of gas made this seem unlikely. All this time I was readying my house to sell; painting here and there, tearing up old carpeting, and gluing peeling wallpaper back on had become my after-work projects, since I was spending most of every weekend searching for that perfect next space.

While I had told my friends that I was looking in the area, I didn't tell them that I'd also decided to look farther afield. I didn't want their "helpful" advice, which might have convinced me to spend more than I wanted in order to remain nearby. My master plan included taking my business online (I'm a career adviser), which would probably decrease my earnings, for a while at least. Or maybe I'd take early retirement and do something else, not knowing what that might be or when it would happen. I didn't want to be persuaded to spend money I had set aside to cover these probable decreases in income. And I wasn't ready to move to California, since I wasn't sure either of my children planned on staying there.

Moving farther away would mean I'd have to start over: meeting new friends, finding my way around, learning what cultural events were available. If I were going to have to do all these things anyway, living only one hour away, then why not look farther—in western Massachusetts or Vermont or even Rhode Island? Looking for a new house or condo became a much bigger project, but also a much more interesting one. I really had to focus on what I wanted. An over-55 community? A freestanding house? A condo—in a small or large complex? Cohousing? So many options to sort through.

I first decided on where to look—the Berkshires in western Massachusetts—and started looking there. I drove the two-and-a-half hours west and had a realtor show me six to eight housing options each week for at least six weeks. My house was on the market at this point, and I wondered whether I'd need a Plan B if I couldn't find the right place to move into before my old place sold. I decided that if I had to rent, I'd do so in Tuscany or Provence. Plan B became as desirable an option as buying and moving, even though I'd have to go through the process again when I no longer wanted to rent. But it just felt good to have that Plan B.

Then serendipity smiled on me. During one of my post-house-hunting journeys back to Boston from western Massachusetts there was an accident on the turnpike and I turned off to circumvent the traffic. I drove through the Pioneer Valley as I made my way back to the highway and thought, "Why am I not looking here?" There was beautiful scenery, five colleges in close proximity, lots of shopping options, and a farm stand down every side road. As soon as I made it home I looked for a realtor in that area. My weekends were now even busier, as one day was spent looking at houses in the Berkshires and the other was spent in the Pioneer Valley looking at still more.

Then one day I got out of my car and knew I'd found the right place—even before I went inside. How did I know? The view from the driveway was one I was already familiar with: it was a scene I'd imagined whenever I did a guided meditation—sitting on a screened porch with mountains ahead, a field to my left, and a few apple trees in the field to my right. And there it was, just as I'd envisioned. The house is a small, three-bedroom ranch with a fireplace and attached garage, the perfect size for one or more guests. The price was actually just below what I'd budgeted, so I would be able to make some minor improvements. The old house sold at about the same time, and my selling realtor let me know that she was a little disappointed that I didn't get to exercise Plan B. Maybe I was, too, a little. On the other hand, I was thrilled with my house in the country and its fabulous view, which changes every day with the weather.

After five years I'm still excited by the decision to move, and I'm still learning my way around (with Siri's help—and a good map). Those friends from the city? They keep visiting me for a break from their regular routines, and we Skype regularly.

Your story will be different. You may even decide to stay where you are—that's a perfectly good option for some. In any case, it's your adventure and I want you to enjoy it. The information in the following pages will help.

This chapter looks at the possible options, giving you an opportunity to begin thinking about and comparing alternate housing choices. Although your options may change because of larger economic as well as personal circumstances, it's a starting place for discussion and further investigation.

MOVE OR STAY?

Often the first decision is the simplest to describe: move or stay? It might be an easy decision because your primary residence no longer suits your needs. Or it may be a challenge to figure out what to do because many factors play into your choice. It's especially important that you not wait too long to make a decision to move if you already expect that your current residence won't serve in your later years. Don't wait until you become too impaired to settle into a new community and make new friends. These adjustments are easier to make when you're younger.

The following checklist can provide some guidance in making the decision to move or stay. Place check marks into the boxes that apply for each statement.

Look at your preferences regarding future housing and compare them to your current situation, and rank them in order of importance. You can weight some of the answers if you feel they are more important than others. If you think your current housing is appropriate for now, then it might make sense to stay until it no longer meets your needs. But if your Future Housing column is filled with check marks, you might consider relocation.

Living where you have friends and neighbors to socialize with and who can help in emergencies is important. Social connections are one of the keys to aging well. Neighborhoods with residents of mixed ages help you stay in touch with current trends. Young adults, teens, and children can often provide a stimulating environment to be involved in as well as potential helpers for hire. But

	CURRENT HOUSING	FUTURE HOUSING	NOT IMPORTANT
Adequate living space			
Outdoor space			
Manageable costs (rent, mortgage, fees, taxes, utilities)			
Finances that can support upkeep and repairs			
Surroundings that can adapt to changing needs (arthritis, wheelchair access)			
Appropriate mobility indoors and out (stairways, single floor, access to bath)			
Sense of security and safety			
Acceptable requirements for maintenance and cleaning			
Place that would accommodate changed circumstances (divorce, death, illness, marriage, children moving in or out)			
Space that allows caring for partner/spouse			
Space that allows caring for parents			
Space that allows caring for children			
Space that allows caring for grandchildren			
Space that allows caring for other family members			
Space that accommodates pets			
Walkable neighborhood			

	CURRENT HOUSING	FUTURE HOUSING	NOT IMPORTANT
Diversity of neighborhood (age and other characteristics)			
Setting—urban, suburban, rural			
Agreeable weather			
Medical needs met (access to doctor, hospital, emergency services)			
Family nearby			
Work and volunteer opportunities nearby			
Access to shopping			
Religious needs met			
Access to cultural and intellectual activities (library, theater, concerts, lectures)			
Public transportation available			
Recreational facilities available (parks, golf courses, beaches, walking trails)			
Natural resources nearby (open space, forests, ocean)			
Educational opportunities available (continuing ed, adult learning)			
Community services available (activity center, tax rebates, public services)			
Opportunities for political and community engagement			

often friends move away and the neighbors change. It's important that you examine *your own needs and wants* before deciding whether to stay where you are. You may want a smaller house but also want to stay in the same ZIP code. On the other hand, a move across town, to the next state, or even across the country, could be the right solution.

What are your current needs? You might want to list them. Then think about your future requirements for health care, transportation, and creating new social networks as you ponder relocation. A home can be located anywhere, at any price. You need to really think hard about what you want as well as what you can do without. Make a list of pros and cons to help with the decision-making—and talk with others about your ideas.

If you know you want to move, but aren't ready just now, take time to consider your options by designing one-, three-, and five-year plans of the actions you'll need to take before moving. These could include home repairs and general tidying and decluttering, along with relocation activities such as learning about the cultural happenings in the areas where you're thinking of moving. It's an opportunity to clean out closets, bureaus, and storage areas and distribute your belongings in an orderly fashion, perhaps as gifts for birthdays or other occasions. If you own your home or condo, you can make repairs or repaint to get it ready to sell, while getting to enjoy these updates yourself for a while. You might give yourself time to find a buyer via word of mouth. Even if you decide to stay, you might still want to create these multiyear plans for upkeep and improvements. They'll give you a head start when it comes to preserving the value of your home and getting ready to sell if circumstances change and moving becomes the better choice for you.

In a November 2010 AARP study, 73 percent of respondents "strongly agree with the statement, 'What I'd really like to do is stay in my current residence for as long as possible.'" This idea of being able to live safely and comfortably in one's own home well into old age has become known as active living. You may be many years away from needing at-home health-related accommodations, but it's worth being aware of issues that may arise and how to deal with them well ahead of time as you think about long-term location decisions. Skim this section now, or start acting on the recommendations if you need to.

According to the 2010 Census, each year more than 3.5 million baby boomers turn sixty-five. In 2015, America's sixty and older population reached 65 million. With this many reaching the age for "aches and pains," home modifications will need to be a serious national concern, as it will be impossible to provide alternative living in retirement communities for so many people.

The first step in determining the possibility of aging in place is to *take stock of your current housing*. Safety concerns are both community and individually based.

Is the neighborhood safe?

Is the house/condo/apartment secure, with securely locking windows and doors?

Are sidewalks/paths kept clear of wet leaves, snow, and other debris?

Can injuries and accidents in the home be eliminated or minimized?

Are emergency personnel available in a timely manner?

How far is it to the nearest hospital?

Do you need to drive to have a social life or to meet basic needs (such as food shopping, entertainment, library)?

Some solutions might involve simple measures such as relocating furniture to make clear pathways through the house, removing throw rugs to minimize slips and falls, or increasing the wattage in light fixtures to provide better visibility. These are small, individual changes that can be easily accomplished. Other safety concerns are beyond the individual (such as ambulance services, city or town responsibility for clearing streets and sidewalks). For a room-by-room guide to potential hazards, see the Home Safety Council's website, MySafeHome.net.

Step two is to request a professional assessment. A new industry is developing around aging in place. Standardization of care is an important goal for any industry player, and you should do a little checking before choosing someone. Some states have certification programs to ensure that individuals, businesses, and agencies which provide elder care are reputable and accountable. CAHSAH, the California Association for Health Services at Home, is one. Geriatric care professionals, occupational therapists, and physical therapists specializing in elder needs can provide on-site assessments and make recommendations and plans for contractors or handymen.

Assessments can include access to the building, ease of movement within the dwelling, and accident prevention measures. Further review of arthritis-related challenges (doorknobs, key locks, hot and cold-water knobs) as well as larger mobility challenges (stairs, doorways, thresholds, bathtubs, and toilet and chair heights) and access (kitchen storage, wheelchair access to sink) are all areas a professional can evaluate.

Once you have an idea of what services you need or want, it's time for step three: determining what services are available. Many communities have councils on aging that can provide information about local agencies and services. Consider which medical, social service, and community-based services (such as transportation, Meals on Wheels, or other services) you want to engage. If there is coordination among agencies or one-stop shopping, there is an opportunity for increased quality and reduced cost.

Home Modifications Aging in place often requires changes to the dwelling. Some modifications can be made inexpensively and easily, such as replacing doorknobs with levers, while others are more complex and expensive. Making wider doorways for wheel-chairs, installing barrier-free bathtubs and showers, or adding stair lifts fall into the pricier category. Compared to the ongoing cost of a nursing home or continuing care facility, however, the investment needed to make changes in your home may be modest and well worth it.

A variety of modifications may be reimbursable through long-term care insurance, and the actual occupational therapy assessment may be covered by health insurance or Medicare. Be sure to check your policy and ask for invoices that indicate the medical necessity for any improvements. In general, long-term care insurance will not pay for upgrades and modifications if you're still healthy. Check out the USC Gerontology Center website for important information (HomeMods.org).

In-Home Technology Medical and health monitoring may be additional needs. Recent inventions can increase the likelihood that you'll be able to remain in your home with daily monitoring and appropriate medical attention. Systems have been designed to collect vital signs such as blood pressure, heart rate, temperature, body weight, and medication levels. These require minimal input by the resident, with data sent via phone line or

Internet connection to a nurse or other health-care professional 365 days per year. Daily monitoring of chronic conditions allows for proactive and preventive care, changes to medication and treatment plans when necessary, and prompt emergency medical responses, if required. Ultimately, interactive medical testing and diagnostic devices can alert doctors to any significant changes that need attention: low blood sugar, signs of a stroke or heart attack, and so on. This kind of monitoring is especially helpful for a single person living alone and for families living at a distance from an older person in need of regular care. It can ease some of the difficult "How are you doing?" conversations that often open family telephone calls.

While in-home monitoring requires some specialized technology, a quick look at the home technology available in general can also aid aging in place. It's important to have access to family, social activities, and community services (such as police or ambulance). Just as you can now start appliances, unlock the door, or turn on lights from your computer or cell phone, automated systems for monitoring seniors are coming on the market. Like baby monitors, there are sensing devices that can alert family members and emergency personnel when there's been a fall or other crisis.

There are also the positive educational and social aspects of being "wired." Online groups, blogs, websites, and social media all offer ways to stay in touch, learn something new, meet new people, and find out about activities. The right technology can help keep people independent and living in their own homes much longer. Look into what's available, find out how other people are using it, and think about how it can help you.

Of course, paying for changes and upgrades may be a barrier to making appropriate modifications. To help, home equity loans, home modification loans, and reverse mortgages are available if you own your home. Talk with a financial professional about these, because there are often high upfront fees, and they may not make sense for your long-term financial security. Check out LongTermCare.gov for additional information.

Naturally Occurring Retirement Communities (NORCs) NORC is a general term for a new movement in supporting older people in their communities and is defined by the Congressional Research Service as "a community with a large proportion of older persons (typically 55+) residing within a specific geographic area"— anything from an apartment complex or condo building to an entire ZIP code. Many residents over fifty-five live in a neighborhood that could qualify as a NORC—just look around. You may already be living in a community that qualifies. New York State, for example, has recognized more than forty NORCs since legislation supporting them was passed in 2006.

NORCs are organized through a mix of public and private partnerships to provide services and activities for their residents. Each of the agencies is already in place, but working cooperatively is a new model. At the core are social service and health-care providers, housing managers, representatives of neighborhood associations, and the residents, especially seniors. But the community partnerships extend beyond the core members to local businesses, civic and religious organizations, and local police.

Beyond offering basic services to individuals, NORC programs promote community change by empowering residents to help shape the communities they live in. Programs are built from the ground up, in response to a community's specific needs. These can include health and social service programs, transportation problems, crime prevention, or addressing a lack of community-based activities. Because they are focused locally, every NORC reflects its own community.

Early NORCs emerged from institutional settings and evolved as effective ways to deliver government-supported services, although fewer than two hundred actually receive government funding for programs and services (free health care, transportation, and so on). The trend is toward recognizing an increasing number of these communities as NORCs. One of the goals for organizing such groups is to find low-cost services that benefit many members of the neighborhood, rather than leaving it to individuals to contract for needed services. Funding for some programs comes from the government or nonprofit groups, most commonly in the case of health care delivered in partnership with a local hospital where the emphasis is on prevention and wellness.

NORCs in affluent communities, often called "villages," may be largely supported by member dues of $500 or more per year. The advocacy of village leaders can result in group rates for home services (such as plumbing and cleaning), neighborhood retail discounts (dry cleaner, exercise classes), and special services, including transportation, shopping, or adult activities and programs. These groups respond to specific community needs determined by a local board of directors, with member participation or input.

If your neighborhood seems to qualify for NORC status, this might be your opportunity to take charge and make it happen. Title IV, Activities for Health, Independence, and Longevity, of the Older Americans Act (OAA), authorizes the awarding of funds, including to private nonprofit agencies and organizations, for training, research, and demonstration projects in the field of aging. Funds can be used to expand knowledge about aging and the aging process and to test innovative ideas about services and programs for older adults. For more information about starting a village in your community, go to NORCblueprint.org and VTV network.org.

Of course, neighborhood collaborations that save residents money can happen in any community—so consider the OAA funding option even if you live in a mixed-age neighborhood. Some ideas for sharing might include snow-blowing, offers to provide childcare in exchange for moving heavy furniture, and the coordination of similar neighborly acts. There is no limit to creative ideas.

Other Options "In-law suites" or accessory apartments can be created in homes that are too big or costly to manage without help. By turning a floor or a section of your home into an apartment, it's possible to generate income, gain companionship, or have help with household tasks. Usually these apartments are separate, private living quarters with at least a mini-kitchen and bathroom. Some even have private entrances. Check the local zoning regulations to see if this is possible in your home.

Sharing your home with a roommate is not just for young people starting out. Elders can benefit from having a roomie, too. Again, having enough private space for each resident is important, but shared kitchen, living, and dining rooms are possible. A good screening process and a thorough understanding of your own needs and set living habits will go a long way toward making a roommate situation work.

ECHO (Elder Cottage Housing Opportunity) dwellings are separate units added in the yard of a single-family home owned by an adult child or other family member. Think "tiny houses." This allows you to live near but not "with" them. Zoning variances are often required for this type of construction, and municipalities sometimes make exceptions for residents over fifty-five. The tiny home concept could be another good option. Special permits might be issued by local agencies on aging. If this seems like a possibility, see what you need to do to make it a reality.

MOVING

Moving is a big deal for most people. Start your research early and be as thorough as possible when exploring the options. Once you decide that you want to move, the next step is deciding where to relocate. Finding a match for your weather, economic, and cultural desires can be fun—like planning a vacation. Type "compare cities" into a search engine and see what pops up: BestPlaces.net, greatplacestoretire.com, and FindYourSpot.com are just a few. Type in the name of your town and a location you've dreamed of to see comparisons of sunny days, museums, nearby restaurants, and real estate possibilities. For cost of living comparisons, visit Salary.com and select the Cost of Living Wizard at the bottom of the home page.

In addition to the basics, you might want to consider:

public transportation options

distance to nearest airport

leash laws or dog parks

nearby health spas and gyms

coffee shops and indie bookstores

proximity to a college or university

bike paths and walking trails

shopping choices

Of course, an online search is only the beginning. Nothing can replace the experience of on-site exploration.

Laura thought Asheville, North Carolina, would be the perfect place to retire after living in Pittsburgh for twenty-three years. She had fallen in love with the area when she'd visited on a spring vacation several years before. Now that her husband had been diagnosed with Parkinson's at age sixty-two, they were ready to make the move to a location with better weather.

She and her husband went to Asheville for a long weekend in January to see what winter was like and to explore the housing market. They were surprised to find snow and ice, though not as much as they'd left behind. As much as she loved the area, now Laura knew that a location farther south or west, with no winter snow, would be a better choice than Asheville.

Taking a cue from Laura's experience, visit your proposed relocation site during a season that's not featured in the travel books. See Florida in August, San Francisco in July, or Seattle in April. If you're interested in a foreign destination, apply the same criteria and visit in the off-season to get a sense of whether (and weather!) it's a dream spot—or a nightmare.

House Single family or multi? Urban, suburban, small town, or rural? North, south, east, west, or somewhere in between? How do you decide? The autonomy of a single dwelling has many advantages. Privacy, decorating preferences, and access to a yard or a garden are just a few. Owning a house can offer a sense of independence and has often been seen as the fulfillment of the American dream.

If you've been living in a house, you may think another house is the right decision. As long as maintenance, taxes, and expenses are not a problem, this can be a good choice. There are growing numbers of services to help with minor handyman jobs as well as ongoing lawn care, transportation services, and meal preparation. If mobility becomes a challenge, it's possible to make some changes to an existing structure when needed.

Owning a house brings the possibility of maintaining or increasing equity (but not always) and leaving the asset as part of your estate. Sometimes financing a purchase can be tricky. There are many options, including a mortgage, outright purchase, or rent-to-buy, for example. Manufactured housing and new construction may have other purchase and financing choices that are not available when you buy an existing home. There's much to explore regarding financing a new home. See the Chapter Resources section of this book for places to start.

There are many online resources to help you investigate houses for sale or rent. Renting may be a better option, at least initially, if you're moving into a new area. By renting you can learn about the new neighborhood and whether it's right for you, without the hassle of having to sell again if you find out that it's not. Keep in mind the IRS time limit if you are selling one home to buy another, which may affect the timing of renting before buying.

Apartment or Condo   Moving from a house to a condo or an apartment may seem like a good idea—there's less space to worry about, maintenance and gardening are provided for, and this kind of dwelling comes with built-in neighbors. Many units have common space—shared facilities such as picnic areas, laundry rooms, and swimming pools—and the building or complex might even have large rooms available for parties or receptions. You can find developments with concierge services, exercise rooms, and their own local transportation, too. Some buildings are high-rise, others multifamily homes; some are in urban and suburban settings near many conveniences, others are part of planned communities. All offer many of the same advantages as a house, but without the responsibility for large-scale improvements and day-to-day maintenance.

Rental apartments can be single-floor, townhouse, or garden-style; sizes range from studio to multibedroom; there can be walk-up or elevator access. The choices are numerous and generally include all regular property maintenance and some utilities in the monthly rent. Becoming good friends with the building's supervisor and the management company can be a big advantage when you need help with plumbing, heat, or noise issues. Rent is determined by the building owners and is subject to change without any input from residents. Leases may or may not be required, but in any case renting allows a quicker turnaround time if you decide to move elsewhere, as you don't need to find a buyer and you can leave at the end of the rental period. By the same token, a rental lease may expire before you are ready to move.

Condo options are equally numerous. The main distinction is that condos are purchased rather than rented (although some owners rent their units to others). Generally, monthly fees cover shared expenses such as water and sewer charges, trash removal, gardening, and exterior maintenance. Management in condo buildings often includes resident participation in shared decision-making, especially when it comes to major expenses. In exploring the condo option, be sure to check on the financial reserves used to finance renovations of common areas, new heating and cooling systems, roof repairs, and other major repairs and improvements. When a condo association has a smaller reserve, it means that individual condo owners will have to cover more of the cost of large projects. Assessments to cover these additional expenses are generally made over several years in the form of increased monthly fees. The cost of utilities and taxes for each unit are the responsibility of each condo owner, just as with a house. All owners become members of the governing association when they purchase their units, and are encouraged to participate in regular meetings and leadership roles. Condo association meetings not only give you the information you need to know about building maintenance and planned spending, but also provide a ready-made social opportunity to meet and get to know your fellow residents. For many women living alone, this is the right solution.

Sandy decided to move into a condo when her husband filed for divorce. She'd always managed a four-bedroom home, but the children had moved out, and she didn't want the memories of good times and bad coloring her new life. What she hadn't anticipated was how excited she was at the prospect of starting over. At sixty-one, she was still working and decided she wanted to shorten her commute. So she looked at two-bedroom condos in a different part of the city, away from close friends and her temple community.

This was the first big purchase Sandy had made on her own. Of course, she'd bought new cars over the years, but her husband had contributed to the decision if not the car loan. This time the decision was all hers. A young, enthusiastic real estate broker wasn't much help. Sandy wanted to know about "senior services" and the profile of the neighborhood, age-wise. She wanted to try to figure out how easy it might be to start over.

Sandy toyed with the idea of renting to see how she might like a new neighborhood, but didn't relish the idea of moving twice. So she did an online search into the demographics of the neighborhoods she was considering. Then she decided to visit several of the small businesses in the area as well as two temples that were nearby. She formulated a list of questions to ask store owners, the rabbis, and people at city hall and the library. The questions were: How would you describe this neighborhood? What do you like best? What do you like least? If you live here, why did you move here? If not, would you move here? Why or why not? And finally, after telling a little about her interests and expectations: Do you think I would like living here?

She also drove around the candidate neighborhoods at various times of the day, on both weekdays and weekends, to see what the traffic was like, as well as to get a feel for the general hustle and bustle on the sidewalks. She was looking for a vibrant community where she would have choices for entertainment, shopping, and being outdoors. The quiet suburban surroundings of her previous home had been fine when she was consumed with raising a family, but now, without PTA meetings and soccer games to meet other people, she wanted a location with more action. She thought, too, that a quaint town might let her easily slip into a hermit-like existence, which she knew might not be healthy. She knew women who had become best friends with Johnny Walker and she didn't want to become another. A neighborhood with "personality" was what she wanted.

It took three months and visits to about twenty available condos before she decided on one. It was in a converted two-family house in a mixed neighborhood: kids and elders; blacks, Asians, Latinos, and whites. The neighborhood included several single-family homes, as well as duplexes and a fourteen-unit apartment building at the intersection a quarter mile away. The streets were clean, yards well maintained, and many gardens extended to the sidewalk. It had a "well cared-for" feeling that Sandy found very appealing. And best of all, when she moved in, the downstairs condo owner had a "welcome to the neighborhood" party, so that Sandy could meet others on the street and they could meet her. It felt like a good beginning to her new life.

Only one consideration spoiled the perfect transition. Because Sandy had purchased the condo before her divorce was finalized, it became part of the total property value with her husband and she lost out on tens of thousands of dollars she would have received from the divorce proceedings if she had rented instead. But for Sandy it was the price she was willing to pay for a new life. Four years later she was the one hosting the "welcome" party for the new condo owner downstairs.

If you've never lived in a multi-unit building, there might be an adjustment period. Hearing neighbors' music through the walls and people walking overhead may be experiences you haven't had since living in a college dorm or in your first apartment long ago, when you might have been more tolerant. On the other hand, you might wish you were better friends with the residents of unit 3C because whatever they're cooking always smells delicious.

If you're away from home on vacation or visiting family or friends, you can feel safer from burglaries because someone is always around. While no dwelling is totally safe from fires or natural disasters, having fellow residents who are always present provides another line of defense and can be a source of support if such a calamity occurs.

The biggest difference is whether you rent or buy. The following information can help you decide.

Rent or Buy?   Whether renting is better than buying depends on many factors, particularly how fast home and condo prices are changing, whether rents are rising, and how long you plan to live there. Here are some things to consider:

If you're planning to live in a home or condo for five years or more, consider buying. If not, renting is likely to be a better option.

What's your anticipated income? If it's not stable and reliable, renting allows you to change your living situation more easily if you need to for financial reasons.

Plan to spend no more than one-third of your income on all housing-related expenses, including rent or mortgage payments, property taxes, insurance, and any other housing-related costs (such as utilities and fees).

Homes and condos for sale and rent can vary both in quality and availability. Be sure to compare all of your options to find your best fit.

Be sure to research the overall economic health of the neighborhood and the larger community. One way is to look for foreclosures and distressed property. You may be able to find great bargains this way, but you might lose property value if you're not careful.

Use the calculators on the following websites to compare the costs of buying and renting. You'll need to include such items as your rate of return on investments, condo fees, and your tax bracket.

nytimes.com/interactive/business/buy-rent-calculator.html

realtor.com/home-finance/financial-calculators/rent-vs-buy-calculator.aspx

realestate.yahoo.com/calculators/rent_vs_own.html

Remember that price, while important, is just one consideration. Location and amenities also factor in, and you may be willing to pay a little more to get what you want and need.

Cohousing The necessary arrangements for unrelated people choosing to live together can be formalized with as little as a legal contract. In one case, several women collaborated to create a "Committee for Retirement Alternatives for Women." They've designed small group settings where they can continue living independently as long as possible, but also remain together to care for one another and bring in additional resources as needed. They agree they'd rather be spending time with friends and the community than be "parked" in a nursing home or be burdens to their families. If you find this idea as appealing as I do, you can find further information at utne.com/housing.

This particular solution is an example of a relatively new option in the United States: cohousing. Originally developed in Denmark, cohousing was promoted in the early 1980s by architects Kathryn McCamant and Charles Durrett. Their idea of an "intentional neighborhood" has spread around the world. Cohousing is potentially a good option for residents of all ages, and elder-specific cohousing communities are now being developed.

Residents actively participate in the creation and operation of their cohousing communities. The design of most communities features one or more pedestrian walks radiating from a common house that hosts a communal dining area, recreational facilities, laundry, guest rooms, and a library or lounge. The neighborhood's homes may either be single-family (attached or freestanding) or consist of a condo or apartment-style building with multiple units. The grounds may incorporate open space, community gardens, and playgrounds, with parking on the periphery. Community members maintain the common property and participate in weekly meals prepared and served in the common house. Some cohousing communities have a mission to "improve the world" either environmentally, politically, or socially.

Because the process of developing a cohousing community takes time, while steps are taken to acquire the land, design the neighborhood, and actually build all the facilities, group members have a chance to get to know their neighbors long before they meet on the front lawn for a chat. This extended process allows people to opt out if they don't feel this is the right housing choice for them.

Moving into an established cohousing community is a little different, but prospective residents usually have to join in at a community meal, attend a group meeting, and perhaps even gain a sponsor from within the community before their application will be accepted. Some communities specify the maximum number of families or single women they'll allow, so that the group retains a mix of ages. This type of community could be a particularly appealing housing option for older singles, but without taking these steps the neighborhood could lose its age diversity over time.

In cohousing developments specifically developed for residents over fifty-five, many designs take into consideration all levels of physical ability and may include accommodations for on-site home health aides who assist residents. Senior cohousing is often developed with universal design principles in mind, so that residents can make the transition from active lifestyles to those requiring mobility accommodations. Both the inside and outside common areas are designed for easy access and all levels of physical recreation. Many elements of senior cohousing allow "aging in place." It's important to remember that while temporary frailty or disability can be managed and supported, intense long-term care is better provided in continuing care facilities. For some, hiring part- or full-time aides is a solution; others will need to move from the community to get the care they need.

If you're interested in starting a cohousing community or moving into one, the Cohousing Association (cohousing.org) has guidelines and resources as well as lists of available homes. Most people move out of cohousing only because their circumstances change, so turnover is low.

Age-Based and Retirement Communities   Sometimes it's more appealing to move to a setting which has been preplanned for older men and women. On-site activities, landscaping and cleaning services, planned excursions, and available transportation make the transition to a new location easier, especially for singles. There's an immediate sense of belonging when you join such a community.

These facilities offer a variety of housing options: individual homes, small unit attached houses, and multi-unit buildings. They often provide other amenities, such as golf courses, swimming pools, clubhouses, group recreational and social activities, and transportation.

Generally, age-based communities limit residents to age fifty-five and older, and some may restrict the length of time children and younger adults can visit with residents. Other communities are more open to younger members, owing to a lack of occupants in the target age range. These communities are designed as neighborhoods, often with social events, holiday parties, book groups, or exercise classes to participate in. Exterior maintenance and landscaping are included in monthly fees. Sometimes there are restrictions and guidelines for "do-it-yourself" projects.

Many of the residences are designed with principles of universal design. Because these communities are often built to accommodate changing needs, they may be flexible enough to allow residents to age in place.

Continuing Care Retirement Communities (CCRCs) or Life Care Communities This choice of housing may only be for affluent seniors, since becoming a resident includes a sizable entry fee and monthly assessments. The independent living charges often cover the costs of skilled care. Independent houses, condos, and townhomes are for the more active seniors, capable of self-managing their everyday needs. Typically, meals are available for all residents as part of the monthly fee, and are served restaurant-style with tablecloths and wait staff.

As a resident's needs change, living spaces also change. Residents who need more services usually move to apartments in a main building, with easy walker and wheelchair access, call buttons for emergency help, and a variety of extra services available, including occupational therapy, medication monitoring, and personal care assistance. Finally, a nursing home's twenty-four-hour care is the third level of housing options.

Most CCRCS emphasize preventive health care, offering immunizations, nutrition guidance, exercise, and physical therapy in the facility, with on-site outpatient clinics for primary care needs and diagnostic testing. Other services can include housekeeping, transportation, and planned social activities.

For a hefty fee, residents in this type of housing have access to a built-in community. There are on-site activities: exercise classes, games, libraries, movies, and other entertainment. Off-site events are often also part of the offerings: excursions to museums, sports events, and concerts, among others.

Currently there are around two thousand CCRCS, according to *USA Today* (October 10, 2014), housing six hundred thousand residents, mostly in independent living. Usually you can enter a CCRC only when you are healthy enough to live on your own. You'll also need to pass a financial test to prove that you won't run out of the money needed to pay the monthly fees. Costs are generally based on the size and features of your housing choice, as well as the amenities and type of care contract you choose.

One little-known tax break exists for CCRC residents. Part of the one-time entrance fee and ongoing monthly fees can be deducted as medical expenses. This is true even for those in independent living. You're allowed to claim a deduction for prepaid medical expense, based on the 2004 Tax Court decision of *Delbert L. Baker v. Commissioner*. The Bakers were able to claim a percentage of their entry fee and their monthly fees as tax deductions. These amounts were calculated on the basis of financial information provided by the nonprofit organization that ran the community.

To claim these benefits, the resident must have a lifetime care contract with the community. Be sure to find out how you or your heirs can get the contract deposit back. And what happens if you run out of money? Sometimes the small print gives the facility the right to collect unpaid fees from your estate. Get advice from a certified public accountant and a lawyer, preferably an eldercare specialist, before signing any contracts.

Take one last important step before you sign on to a lifetime in a CCRC: check the financial status of the facility. You don't want the place to go into foreclosure while you're still a resident. To check on the solvency of a single facility or a chain, go to carf. org, the website for the group that accredits CCRCs. Free reports are available to download, including, the "Consumer Guide to Understanding Financial Performance and Reporting in CCRCs." Another guide, "The Continuing Care Retirement Community: A Guidebook for Consumers," can be downloaded from aahsa. org. Beyond these reports, obtain a copy of the facility's most recent audited financial statements. If they are unwilling to provide them, take note of this and look elsewhere. You can give these reports to your tax professional to review if you don't feel savvy enough to understand them. There should also be a residents' finance committee. It would be a good idea to talk with someone from that group as well.

As with any retirement community, you'll also want to ask about management, staff, activities, and other items of particular interest to you. You'll be spending a lot of money and time at such a facility. You should make sure it will be a good fit for your wants and needs.

International Living   The allure of living in Ireland, the south of France, Guatemala, or somewhere else you've dreamed of seems ideal for retirement. But the dreaming is more prevalent than the actuality. Only about 1 percent of Social Security payments are sent to beneficiaries outside the United States. But that number may be increasing as several factors which once were deterrents are changing. Lower costs and better weather have traditionally been the reasons to locate elsewhere. Those beautiful surroundings, lovely climate, and—yes—lower costs of living are still part of the allure. But some big deal breakers of the past are less so now.

Improved medical care, including medical tourism, has helped debunk some of the negative stereotypes about foreign doctors and hospitals. Medicare does not cover foreign health-care costs, but the low cost of living in many regions can also mean lower medical costs than in the United States. Globalization and the spread of technology have reduced the fears of poor care in many locales around the world, at the same time that the rising cost of US health care makes retiring outside the United States more desirable. It's not an irrevocable decision; you can always return stateside for important operations and other extensive medical care.

While moving to Europe, Central or South America, Africa, Australia, or Asia in times past meant not seeing family and friends very frequently, communication advances make where you live much less relevant. Living in Arizona or Florida might not be so different from living in Spain. Internet access, email, and Skype allow virtual visits anywhere—either by inexpensive phone calls or live cameras on phones or other electronic devices. Air travel is easier, too, and often not too different distance-wise. Visits to see you may be more frequent or longer because you're in an exotic place.

The world is shrinking. While your French may not be *au courant*, technology again comes to the rescue with online translators, GPS-based directions, and restaurant reviews. And many more people speak English, making foreign relocation easier. Some countries even have large expat populations (Mexico and Panama, for example), which can make you feel as though you haven't really left home. The real appeal of international living, though, is learning about another culture and way of life. If you're interested in settling in another country, you might consider living there for three months or more before buying real estate. That way you can get to know the local customs and lifestyles. For more information about living abroad in retirement, go to the websites ExpatInfoDesk.com/expat-guide/retiring-abroad/best -places and InternationalLiving.com.

Another consideration in the offshore equation is tax liability. Be sure to check with a financial professional about your responsibilities for taxes both in the United States and the foreign locale. While your money may go farther elsewhere, you can't shun your obligations as a US citizen. Obtaining foreign citizenship is something else to investigate if you change your residence permanently.

Finally, the populations of many countries around the world are already older than the US population (Japan comes to mind immediately). You're more likely to find countries that take considerations for elder needs into account, as well as cultures that respect their older citizens in Europe and Asia, where they are already adapting to the reality of an older population. Better handicapped access to buildings and abundant elder seating on buses and subways are just two easily observed accommodations for an aging population. If you have wanderlust and are ready for an adventure, head overseas to explore a few of these options for yourself.

SOME FINAL THOUGHTS

Whether a suburban bungalow, a country cottage, a city apartment, or a tree house, there's no place like home. Housing often consumes the biggest share of monthly expenses: rent or mortgage, taxes, insurance, heating and cooling, repairs, updates, utilities, and furnishings. But living on the streets or in a tent usually isn't a good alternative. Where you live is a big factor in creating a satisfying life.

Sometimes the best-made plans fall apart. A spouse or partner gets sick or dies. Children and their families move away. Or parents who live elsewhere now need care. Maybe it's too much traffic, snow, or high taxes that lead to thoughts of moving. Living arrangements that work when we're healthy may not fit our needs if we become physically, visually, or mentally disabled—or just less capable.

If you're still working, there are other considerations. Do you, or can you, work from home? If so, your choices of housing options are limited only by your resources. But if you still need to go to an office, you're less likely to relocate to a self-standing retirement haven at some distance from your workplace. If you must move, how easily can you find a job in the new location?

If you want to downsize or go a little greener, you can find housing to fit those desires. Many urban areas are starting to cater to older populations with transportation and housekeeping services that make aging in place or staying put a more viable possibility. Or would you prefer small-town living or wide-open spaces?

Whatever the reason, choosing where to live, whether to rent or buy or move in with family members, is a big decision. What have your friends' and family's experiences been with moving or staying in place? Talk with them to learn what they found most challenging. Interview them to uncover the factors they didn't consider, but which turned out to be major issues, both pro and con. If you decide to move, think about those possessions you want to take with you. Your current furniture may be larger than the new rooms can accommodate. And if you're downsizing, there may be just too many beds, bureaus, and other items to take along. No family dispute can be as emotional as the one in which siblings battle over Aunt Edna's china or Grandpa's model boat collection, so be ready to deal with these squabbles.

Remember, if you do move and it isn't right, consider moving again. You'll be wiser and have a clearer idea of what your needs are—and what you'd prefer to do without. By the same token, if you choose to stay where you are and things don't work out as you'd planned, you can always move later.

BECOME A HOUSING ADVOCATE

There are many opportunities to get involved in elder care issues at the local, state, and federal levels. Demand for private and public services for older people is increasing every year. Advocating for these needs while you're still young and active will contribute to improving the choices for you and others. In general, the elderly are an underrepresented group when decisions are made for both services and funding. Become vocal and help make change happen.

6 DOLLARS AND SENSE · PLANNING FOR UNCERTAIN TIMES

A big part of financial freedom is having your heart and
mind free from worry about the what-ifs of life.
—Suze Orman, *The Nine Steps to Financial Freedom: Practical
and Spiritual Steps So You Can Stop Worrying*

Don't worry. This chapter is not about investment choices, nor is
it about how to create an estate or retirement plan. You'll need
advice from legal and financial professionals for those things.
No, this chapter will give you information to ask the right questions when you meet with the pros. It will also give some background info on what financial literacy is and why it's so critical
for women. Why is it so critical? We probably did less paid work
because we were providing child or elder care, which means we
contributed less to our retirement accounts, whether Social Security, a pension, 401(k), 403(b), or a self-employed plan (formally, a
simplified employee pension, or SEP). We probably also earned
less than our male counterparts during the years we were working, so our nest eggs are smaller. If those reasons aren't enough,
we live longer, so we have more need for retirement funds.

We often provide end-of-life care for spouses, too. What that
can lead to is a serious lack of funds when we're the ones who need
care. Whatever savings were available often get spent on medical
care for the first spouse, leaving little or nothing for the survi-
vor. That's not fair. Current Medicare and Medicaid resources are
spent on institutions (hospitals, rehab, nursing homes), although
a large percentage of care occurs at home. Legislative change to

provide more funds for home care and daily needs is not likely as long as lobbyists have the ear of Congress. But the reality is that there are not enough nursing homes for the number of baby boomers who will need their services.

If you can, include home health-care costs in your long-term financial plan. That may mean buying a long-term care insurance policy that includes daily rates for home care. Or it may mean putting aside money in a trust for the surviving spouse, usually the wife, so that she is not left destitute. Now that you know why you need a financial plan, let's step back a bit and figure out what you need to know in order to create a plan that will work for you.

First and foremost is a willingness to learn about financial subjects: income streams, investments, insurance, budgets, IRAs, RMDs (required minimum distributions), and other related topics. It might not be easy or fun, but it's essential to your survival in your later decades. No one is as interested in your money as you are. Scams happen because targets aren't as informed as they should be. It's not too late to learn about Social Security, reverse mortgages, annuities, and other relevant subjects. In fact, learning about money is a never-ending process because of constant changes in the law and new investment opportunities. There are online courses, classes at senior centers, and continuing education programs. End-of-life bankruptcy is a very real possibility for those who are unprepared, so do what you can to avoid it and its consequences.

To get started, you may have to change some long-held beliefs about money. Money is only a means of exchange. It has no magic in itself, but beliefs can color your attitude and willingness to have it, keep it, and learn about it. What's important about money to you? Happiness, independence, helping others? Power, peace of mind, fun, adventure? Love, control, a measure of success, a cause of anxiety? These are emotional values you put on money.

How you feel about money will translate into your personal set of financial goals. These may include paying bills on time, having no debt, traveling, donating, investing, budgeting, helping family or friends, or staying independent as long as possible. Or something else uniquely yours to decide.

I hope you're starting to understand the importance of creating a financial plan that meets your needs and desires in the years ahead. Many of us did not manage the money in our marriages, and found out the hard way that the prince was not around for "happily ever after." Or that widowhood, in addition to grief, left taxes to be filed, bills to be paid, and a big question about what to do next with bank accounts, insurance coverage, and investments. Single women may have an advantage, since they've probably been managing their own finances for some time.

Anxiety about math sometimes adds to the burden of making sound financial choices. I'm sure you've overcome other life challenges, so you can also be successful in managing your money and other resources as well. Let's begin.

INCOME AND OUTGO

First, gather information. That means income as well as spending. If this sounds a lot like creating a budget, you shouldn't feel any surprise there. If you're a regular budgeter this task will be easy—just gather your records. If you avoid budgeting, as I do, then the task is a little more complicated. Start with your income. What are the sources: paycheck, Social Security, pension, investment dividends, annuity payouts, alimony? Think of all the automatic payments as well as checks or cash you receive. This is the easy part.

Once you know where the money's coming from, you then discover where it all goes. Gathering this information might be the hardest part. Here are some items to consider.

HOUSING	Rent or mortgage	Property taxes
	House maintenance costs or HOA fees	Utilities
	Homeowner's / renter's insurance	

LIVING	Groceries and household products	Eating out
	Transportation	Gas
	Car maintenance	Car insurance
	Excise tax	Credit card debt
	Travel / vacations	Hobbies
	Gifts	Charitable donations

MEDICAL	Health insurance	LTC insurance
	Medical expenses (doctor, dentist, optician)	Medications
	Medical supplies (including eyeglasses)	

PERSONAL	Clothes	Personal care (haircuts, pedicures)
	Alimony payments	Adult day care / special services
	Education	

OTHER	Music lessons	
	Memberships	
	. . . and so on	

There are many budget worksheets available online, and some also include retirement calculators. There are printable pdf forms and other tools you can complete on your computer. See Kiplinger.com, getsmarteraboutmoney.ca, mint.com, bankrate. com, *USA Today*, and *CNN Money*, for example. Many of the investment companies also have online calculators. Try Vanguard, T. Rowe Price, Fidelity, and AARP. Analyzenow.com has more complex planning tools, if you're up for it.

Now you have the first parts of a budget and planning tool. The info you've gathered is based on facts. The next phase of the process requires both facts and best-guess estimates as you project into the future. What will be your income sources in the future? How will your expenses be different? Those are the key questions that need to be answered so that you can create a realistic plan.

It can be hard to identify what expenses may crop up, but here are a few items that could disrupt your finances in a big way:

Too many costly vacations. What counts as "too many" for one person can be quite different for another. Just be aware that with more free time people often plan to travel. Be sure to consider the long-term financial implications when you're booking that flight to Australia or that cruise around the Caribbean.

Starting, or resuming, an expensive hobby. These expenses might get out of hand in the early years just because the time to pursue them is now available. The cost of golfing several times a week can be significant. The same is true if you decide to start collecting antiques or playing the piano. All are possible; just be mindful of the costs involved, and plan for them.

Home improvements can take a chunk of cash. Those rooms the kids no longer use can become craft centers with new bookshelves, carpeting, and better lighting. Or the kitchen that you coped with for so long seems terribly outdated and in need of a makeover now that you're around to spend more time fixing meals. Or maybe the improvements are in preparation for declining mobility. All are legitimate reasons to make changes, but don't go into debt in the process. This is not the time for a home equity loan or second mortgage. If you don't want to move to get the changes you desire, then plan to save up until you have the funds. You may decide the kitchen works just fine after all.

Bailing out an adult child can cause a huge financial drain. Monthly allowances to pay off student loans or because of unemployment probably cannot be regained in the current low-interest economy. Of course you want to help your children and let them move back in after a divorce or job loss. Or buy them a home or pay their rent. But all these costs put your own future in jeopardy. Will they be able to pick up the slack when you need it?

And if the kids don't need you, maybe a parent does. Helping with their household maintenance bills or paying for care can add up. They may end up moving in with you or require nursing home care. Of course you can't say no, but you should be aware of your own needs as you make these decisions. With luck, your parents planned for these contingencies and the burden will not fall to you.

Supporting a special-needs child or other family member never ends. Your financial plans may include setting up a trust or purchasing life insurance where the proceeds cover their care when you are gone.

Increased taxes. This is often a surprise, but when you start living off the proceeds of your investments—such as IRAs and 401(k)s—you may find you owe more taxes than when you were working. Also, capital gains tax rates are different from earned-income rates. Don't be shocked when you have quarterly tax obligations that you never worried about because taxes were automatically deducted from your paycheck. Being mindful of your financial obligations may be something new. It's an important part of creating a workable financial plan.

Those are just some of the more common expenses that may be unexpected, but can be planned for.

One expense that will rise over time is the cost of health care. How much and when the increases will come are hard to predict. Injuries from a car accident could be extensive and happen at any time. A chronic condition could flare up and require hospitalization or rehab. Sure, Medicare will cover many of these expenses, but there are limits, and there are services that are not covered. If you can afford to pay unexpected bills using your savings, then you don't need to worry. For those of us who can't, some insurance might be the answer. Long-term care (LTC) insurance may be a solution, but even that has limitations and restrictions. Having some money set aside for health needs in a financial plan makes sense. How much? That's a hard question to answer. Think about your current health status and your family medical history to make a guess about what you'll need, and try to set it aside for a rainy day.

DO YOU NEED A FINANCIAL PLANNER?

It's probably become obvious that planning your financial future has many moving parts. Unless you're a financial whiz, I'd recommend getting help. People with modest savings and income can benefit from professional help, even if it's only to create an outline for the future. It's a good investment regardless of your circumstances. There are many people who offer financial advice. It is very important to choose wisely.

Just as with your doctor, you want a financial planner you feel comfortable with and who gives good advice for your needs. Many brokerage houses (Fidelity, Vanguard, and others) and insurance companies (like Prudential, MetLife, and AARP) offer free financial planning services. But buyer beware: companies generally offer only their own products as the solutions in your financial plan. They make commissions on their offerings and may recommend products that are not the best choices for you, but generate the highest commissions. To avoid these conflicts of interest, choose instead an independent financial planner who is paid on a fee-for-service basis or who earns a percentage of the resources she manages (just be certain that percentage isn't too high). These professionals, acting in a fiduciary capacity, are more likely to have your best interests in mind when making recommendations.

How do you find a qualified financial planner? Ask trusted friends and relatives whether they recommend their planners. This is a time to look for someone who has many women as clients, because investment risks and life expectancy, as well as possible lower asset levels, can determine a different planning strategy than for the typical man.

If you don't get any reliable recommendations, you'll need to shop around. The most endorsed source to consult is the National Association of Personal Financial Advisors (napfa.org) where you can search for a planner by ZIP code or name. From there you can visit individual websites to find out more. Here is the basic information you should gather:

What training does she have? CFP (Certified Financial Planner) is the most rigorous. Chartered Financial Consultant (CFC) is an insurance broker.

What kind of planning does she do? Comprehensive planning includes retirement and investment planning, of course. But a planner should also be able to talk about tax planning, education funding, risk management, and estate planning. Even if not an expert in all these fields, she should work with other professionals to give you what you need for effective and comprehensive financial planning. Tax planning and estate planning are very important financial considerations as we age—even for people of modest means.

How long has the adviser been practicing? Has she had experience with retirement distribution planning? This is essential for creating a successful financial plan in old age.

How many clients does the planner have and what kind? Individuals, small business, nonprofits? The ideal planner has enough experience with many people like you, but doesn't have so many clients that your needs get pushed aside.

Is the adviser part of a larger organization or is she an individual practitioner?

There are no correct answers to these questions: what meets your needs and preferences is the deciding factor. A comprehensive list of questions can be found at the Certified Financial Planner Board of Standards website, plannersearch.org, and includes a section to learn more about choosing a CFP.

Nothing substitutes for an in-person interview, however. The adviser should be willing to spend at least half an hour learning about your needs and explaining her expertise. Have detailed information ready for the appointment. Like visiting a doctor, this is the checkup on your financial health. Be honest about your assets and liabilities—what you own and what you owe. Have some idea of what you want for the future: lifestyle, housing, what you might want to leave to your children or charities. Then listen to hear if the adviser understands you. If you're uncomfortable with the communication style (too much jargon, for example), consider seeking another adviser. You need to understand each other to provide workable financial plans.

If cost is a factor in seeking financial help, many senior centers offer financial planning advice for free or with low fees. Also, many communities have low-cost continuing education classes that are led by financial advisers. Just be aware they may represent insurance companies or brokerages. It's even worth asking a fee-for-service financial adviser if she has a sliding scale or package pricing.

Just before Carole was planning to retire at sixty-six, she became concerned that she couldn't live on Social Security and decided she needed a financial plan. She was referred to a CFP by a good friend. When she explained that she didn't have much money and was worried about the fee, the CFP offered her an option of meeting and creating a simple plan for a fixed fee rather than her usual hourly rate. Carole was relieved that she could get an expert's advice for a reasonable amount. And she's glad she did.

After reviewing Carole's income, 401(k), savings, and expense information, the CFP told Carole she should not retire until age seventy, and that she should start living below her means immediately. Fortunately, Carole paid off her credit card each month and was renting, so she had no debt. Even her car was paid off. The initial conversation and plan showed Carole that she'd need to find less expensive housing when she was no longer working. Also, she should start saving for a new car to be purchased in three years.

Fast forward to age sixty-eight. Carole was let go from her job when her employer sold the business. Retirement arrived earlier than planned! Carole returned to the CFP, and they devised a new plan. It was time to move, so Carole applied for subsidized housing in the Detroit suburb where she'd been living for over twenty years. But before that was available, a friend who'd retired to Florida with her husband suggested that Carole move there. She investigated that option and eventually chose it. As for the financial plan, the 401(k) moved to a brokerage firm, and a new retirement investment account was set up for the required minimum distributions that started last year when she turned seventy-and-a-half. She's been managing to live on her Social Security, so she decided not to take the distributions directly. When Carole's ninety-three-year-old mother, who had been living in a Medicaid-funded nursing home, passed away, Carole was surprised to inherit a $10,000 savings account. It provides just the cushion she needs to make payments on a new car and visit her daughter on the West Coast twice a year. And since the brokerage account was responsible for the 401(k) distribution, she worked directly with them to determine what should be done with the funds.

Carole doesn't feel the need for a new financial plan, but is happy she had a clear idea of what her financial situation would be after she stopped having a regular paycheck. She's now working six hours each week for her church. That $300 a month pays for dinners out with friends as well as her Netflix and Hulu memberships, and she even puts a little into the rainy day fund she opened at her credit union with her inheritance.

"I've always led a simple life," she remarked, "so it's not really that hard not to spend money I don't have."

Carole's biggest surprise? "That I'm living off Social Security and my life is fine. Just as long as I stay healthy."

If Carole can do it, so can you. The secret is to have a plan and then follow it, making adjustments as circumstances change.

INSURANCE: WHAT KIND? HOW MUCH?

As we age, long-term care coverage may seem the most important insurance to have. But what about life insurance? Or longevity insurance? Or funeral and burial expense insurance? Finding complete answers to these questions is another reason to seek help from a professional financial planner. But here is an abbreviated explanation of some more common types of insurance and what to look for and avoid.

In general, you should seek an insurance broker, not an insurance agent. A broker represents many companies and can offer a wide selection of products. An agent works for one company and only sells its products. This applies to purchasing all types of insurance you might want.

LONG-TERM CARE INSURANCE

Do you need it? Can you afford it? Will it do what you want? It depends. The policies available today do not match the extensive provisions that were included when these products were first introduced. If you were foresighted enough to purchase a policy in the 1990s, do not let the premiums lapse. You cannot replace the options you have. If you're considering LTC insurance, buy it when you are as young as possible, but probably not before age sixty. Annual premiums are based on age. That means you'll pay less per year the younger you start, but LTC insurance is not inexpensive.

LTC covers in-home health care, nursing homes, and rehab facilities, and will kick in after standard Medicare coverage has expired. The most important item to purchase is the $/day coverage for home health aides, adult day care, and home-delivered meals, as well as payments to facilities providing care. The $/day feature allocates a certain amount of money for care each day, but if the money is not all used, it can be carried over, thus extending your benefit. The average need for care is currently about three years, according to reviews.com (January 20, 2017). If you cannot afford to pay for three years of coverage, then two years is still useful. Try to find a policy that uses calendar days in the elimination period (usually ninety days). Inflation protection is also important, according to the *Wall Street Journal* (December 10, 2016), unless you're over seventy-five. While $100 a day may seem like adequate coverage today, when you need services in ten years, that probably will not be enough.

Other important considerations with LTC coverage are who determines when you're eligible for benefits and whether mental function is part of the evaluation for eligibility. Most important, get everything in writing! Request it if it's not offered. If you don't understand everything, have an attorney read it and explain the terms. This is a contract, after all. Regardless of how much time and effort you put into choosing your policy, be prepared for disputes to your claims. Keep all receipts and records that might be required for filing a claim.

Policies are costly and vary from state to state. To find estimates for your location, check out genworth.com, which lists costs for home care, day care, and nursing homes. This can help you determine the total amount of coverage you'll need. See what services Medicare covers and tailor your LTC plan to complement that. It's important to find an independent broker to answer your questions. Family and friend referrals are the places to start to find a salesperson. If you need resources, the National Association of Insurance and Financial Advisors (naifa.org) or the National Association of Health Underwriters (nahu.org) are good choices to begin with. Remember to check out the credentials and history of anyone you want to work with.

If you can afford it, LTC insurance is a valuable part of your financial plan.

LIFE INSURANCE

Do you need it? Here are some questions to ask that can help you decide:

> When you die, will someone experience a financial loss? If a spouse will still receive a steady source of income to cover her or his needs, then no insurance is needed.

> Do you want life insurance? Perhaps you like the idea of providing benefits for family or a favorite charity at your death. If so, then yes.

> How much do you need? Enough to pay off the mortgage? Several years' worth of income? These amounts, or what you would like to leave for family or donations, should guide your decision. Maybe yes and maybe no.

> How long will you need insurance? You may have had insurance during your working years or those of a spouse. If you have a nest egg that will provide for your needs, you can cancel or choose to continue the policy. For a new policy, you may only need to cover income losses until your retirement income kicks in. So either yes or no.

If you've decided you want life insurance, what type of life insurance should you buy? For just closing the gap before retirement, term insurance is fine. If you own a small business you might want a permanent life policy that will give your heirs cash to pay taxes rather than sell the business to get the funds. A universal policy is also the choice if you want to benefit a charity or cover your final expenses. Universal, permanent, or whole life (all names for this kind of policy) is a costlier insurance to buy than term.

But you may not need life insurance at all. This is a question that should be answered with your financial adviser or lawyer. There are a variety of circumstances where life insurance would be useful and others where the cost of coverage doesn't make sense. Every case is unique.

LONGEVITY INSURANCE

What is it? Longevity insurance is a deferred annuity, designed to provide income once a policyholder reaches a certain age. You typically purchase this at age sixty-five for payouts starting at age eighty or eighty-five. Unused funds may be left to beneficiaries. Generally, there is a one-time payment. You can use up to 25 percent or $125,000 of an IRA or 401(k) to purchase a qualifying longevity annuity if you don't have ready cash.

While a single premium annuity would begin paying as soon as the account is established, the longevity annuity does not begin payments until the designated age. At current rates, and considering 3 percent inflation, a payout equivalent to $30,000 today would require a single premium investment of $250,000, according to financial planner Michael Kitces (kitces.com). This would supplement Social Security and provide peace of mind if there were a health emergency that required significant funds from your financial resources.

Longevity insurance doesn't make sense for everyone. If your savings are large enough that you don't fear outliving your money, there's no need for this. And if you have a life-threatening illness and probably won't live until the payout period, this is not a good investment. If, however, you have a family history of relatives living into their nineties, you are a good candidate. Be aware of these possible pitfalls with a longevity annuity: there is no inflation adjustment, no death benefit, and no early access to the funds once they're invested. As with all insurance and annuity products, you need to see how they fit into your comprehensive financial plan.

FINANCIAL VERSUS ESTATE PLANNING

Your estate includes everything you own: car, home, investments, furniture, jewelry, and so on. Deciding what will happen to all these things, as well as instructions for your care if you become physically or mentally disabled, is included in estate planning. Financial plans determine how you will live your life, while estate plans determine what happens when you die. An effective estate plan will minimize taxes, legal fees, and court costs. It can include instructions for distributing personal items, as well. And via living wills, trusts, and health and financial powers-of-attorney (if you become incapacitated), your estate plan provides guidance on how you want yourself and your assets to be treated.

Estate planning is for everyone. And it is not a one-time event. Your family and financial situation can change over time—as can the laws. If you don't have a plan, your state does: if you die without an intentional estate plan, your assets will be distributed according to state probate laws. This may not reflect your desires.

An estate plan starts with a will or a living trust. Any assets in your name or directed by your will must go through probate court, often taking nine months to two years, with court and legal fees attached. But not everything must be probated. Any jointly owned property or beneficiary-assigned assets (life insurance, IRAs, 401(k)s, annuities, and the like) are outside the will.

Another alternative to a will is a revocable living trust. It brings all your assets together into one place, can avoid probate at death, and can be changed at any time. It is more expensive to set up a living trust, but many people see the advantages over a will as a bargain.

Start your estate planning with a will and power-of-attorney for health care and financial decisions. Forms are available online, but working with an attorney is worth the investment. If you need a referral, ask your friends, family, and financial planner. Check the National Elder Law Foundation (nelf.org) as another resource.

So now that you realize you need an estate plan, how do you get started? Estate planning can be an emotionally charged activity. After all, you are deciding how to divide your assets after your death. To get started, you need to get organized and gather information, of course. Here are some documents you'll need to have available:

investments, including stock certificates and online accounts

insurance policies, including annuities

bank accounts, safety deposit boxes, associated access information, and keys

car titles

mortgage documents

IRA, 401(k), and pension information

previous wills and trust documents

old tax returns to help identify all assets

In today's electronic world, it's important also to include any online accounts, with their usernames, passwords, and PINs.

This is also a time to determine who should be the executor, as well as to set up powers-of-attorney for health and finances and, if you want, an advanced directive for end-of-life decisions. Conversations about all these topics should be held every few years, rather than during a crisis, if possible. Explaining your plans and wishes can keep the lines of communication open among family members and provide you an opportunity to explain your thinking. If you have children, talk with each of them about their inheritance separately. Find out what they expect and want. You'll learn where the conflicts might be. Don't mislead them. You don't want them to find out at your death that you gave away Aunt Martha's engagement ring to a cousin when your daughter was expecting it. Surprises can lead to contentious relationships. Sometimes it's not easy to have these discussions, since they bring up the topic of your death, but conducting them in a calm manner before a crisis can make them more pleasant.

THE OTHER SIDE OF INDIVIDUALISM

The traditional belief in economic self-sufficiency may deter changes in legislation to cover the social needs of the future. Too few have saved enough to cover their extended life needs, and costs continue to rise. This includes legislation for continued Social Security benefits, which for many older women are the only source of income.

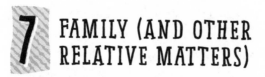

7 FAMILY (AND OTHER RELATIVE MATTERS)

Being a grownup means assuming responsibility for yourself, for your children, and—here's the big curve—for your parents. In other words, you do get to stay up later, but you want to go to sleep earlier.
—Wendy Wasserstein, *Bachelor Girls*

We've all lived our lives within the context of a family—as daughter, sister, mother, grandmother, aunt, or wife—that may be biological or created. Family includes:

Those you inherit—parents, siblings, cousins, and in-laws

Those you choose—friends, lovers, companions, and spouses

Those you raise—children, grandchildren, and others who have benefited from your love and attention

The emotional connections may be strong or weak, but they affect us throughout our lives. There's a constant exchange of care, guidance, financial support, and affection within families. Sometimes you initiate the interaction and sometimes you're the recipient.

One advantage of growing older is the ability to reconsider our relationships. It's a time to clear toxic people out of our lives, which is sometimes easier said than done, but it's necessary for our own well-being in many instances. It's also a time to reconnect with family who may have become estranged over time. The chance to look back and reevaluate relationships is one of the positives of aging. There usually is a chance to mend fences, if you're so inclined. Families, however they're defined, are important relationships.

Probably the most important thing that families can do is spend time together just relaxing or engaging in activities they enjoy. Sharing stories and acknowledging what makes each family member special enhances the sense of belonging.

Holidays are often the time when families are together. Holidays can be great times to reconnect, and these gatherings often are multigenerational. Although there are several movies depicting the stress and strain of holiday get-togethers, it can be a nice time to share long-standing family traditions or to start new ones. Setting realistic expectations and having a forgiving attitude can go a long way toward creating happy celebrations of being together. Even the disasters, when they happen, can become fodder for laughter at future gatherings.

Tensions often arise when multiple generations with different ideas of appropriate behavior interact. Unlike members of perfect TV families, who rarely argue (and if they do, the problem is solved by the end of the episode), real families often disagree. Frequently these disagreements arise across generations. The strength of the relationship can often predict the outcome of any dispute. Some families are emotionally close and have frequent contact with one another, even if they don't live near one another. They stay emotionally close by visiting, making phone calls, and exchanging email. They more or less know what is going on in one another's lives. They care for one another across generations, reaching out in emergencies and during longer term illnesses, and they are somewhat tolerant of opposing views among family members. Other families consider themselves close, but don't visit often and frequently live at some distance from one another. They are somewhat tolerant of opposing views and are more likely to depend on people outside their family for care for long-term needs. They probably will rally for emergencies. Some families feel obliged to provide support and care to family members, but don't feel emotionally close to one another. They may live at some distance from one another or have long-term family conflict that keeps them apart. In emergencies they may rally, but for long-term care there may be resentment over their sense of obligation. They are also less forgiving of one another. And finally, there are detached families whose members don't see one another often and don't support or care for one another. This may be a temporary issue that resolves itself when a crisis arises, or it may be permanent. All of these relationships usually develop over time, although attitudes toward family can be inherited—hearing that "great-aunt Nancy cannot be trusted" for years before even meeting her will shape a relationship. Divorce may cause strained relations with adult children and their families, who may become detached from one or even both parents. An adult child's divorce can also change the relationship dynamics between grandparents and their grandchildren.

If you become the matriarch of your family, it may be up to you to create and maintain positive family interactions. You may be lucky and have the support of a like-minded spouse. Maybe you're divorced or widowed, which can add more complex emotional challenges to the family dynamic. If you're recently widowed, the support of other widows will be most useful. Over time, however, you'll probably rely more on children, friends, and other relatives for support. It takes time to understand your new role in the family and social circle.

Your divorce can also rearrange the family dynamic. It's up to you to decide if you want to maintain any ties to your ex's family members. Your siblings and children will have adjustments to make, too. Be patient and available to talk and listen to any of their concerns. And if you decide to remarry, be ready for the possibility of fireworks instead of support. Again, family dynamics are in flux: there may be a whole new family to incorporate into holiday plans. Not only emotional but financial issues may arise. Who will get what property, asset, or heirloom, now that a second spouse and possibly stepchildren have been added to the equation? Maybe it's better not to tie the knot and just live together instead!

ADULT CHILDREN

Probably one of the biggest challenges of family dynamics is re-negotiating the relationship with adult children. It can be hard to let go of old patterns of communication and expectations. But it's up to you to be the grownup. Your willingness to refrain from telling your child what to do or how to do it is a great first step. And no "I told you so," either. It's hard to move away from being the parent. Sometimes it's easier if you don't live too close or communicate too often—at least until you've mastered the art of interacting adult-to-adult instead of parent-to-child. Part of that transition is helped if you first know what your expectations are, so that you then can communicate them to your child. Because each child may have different expectations (if you have multiple children), plan on addressing each set of expectations differently, depending on your relationship. What do they expect from you? It is a two-way street, after all, as you move from being the parent to being the parent of an adult child.

It's usually a harder adjustment if your adult child moves back home. If you're living under the same roof, it's natural to slip back into old roles and behaviors. It's likely that either you or your child, or both, resent the fact that they are not living on their own.

This might be a short stay, or it might extend to several years. It's important that you set some guidelines and ground rules at the start. Be sure that everyone agrees on the rules, so that things can move forward as smoothly as possible.

Cathy and Dave thought that their children had moved out, since both were married and living on their own. So imagine their surprise when Brad asked if he and his wife, Zoe, could move in, so that they could save for a down payment on a house. Even though both were working, paying the increasing rent for their Los Angeles apartment made it hard to save. The four of them sat down and discussed the possibilities: giving Brad and Zoe a monthly allowance to help cover their rent; converting the family room off the kitchen into a bedroom, while adding a shower to the half bath and allowing use of the kitchen; or letting Brad and Zoe sleep in Brad's old bedroom and use the rest of the house. There were pros and cons to all the options, of course. In the end, Cathy and Dave decided that adding a shower to the bathroom would increase the value of their home and would offer more privacy to both couples, since then the only conflict might arise over using the kitchen, as opposed to using the rest of the house together. What wasn't finalized was how long this arrangement would be in place. Cathy wanted to set a time limit to encourage the young couple to save as much as they could, but Dave thought it would be good to have someone in the house when he traveled for work, and wasn't concerned about how long they stayed.

Seventeen months later, Brad and Zoe moved into a fixer-upper. Cathy was actually a little sad to see them go, since both of them had helped around the house and garden, an unexpected bonus. It had been a surprisingly easy arrangement, as both Brad and Zoe spent long hours at work and often ate out. There was less conflict than Cathy had anticipated around using the kitchen. As a thank-you, the kids gave Cathy and Dave a puppy from the animal shelter. Cathy's not so sure she needed company!

Probably the most important issue in multigenerational households is privacy. If there is any way you can help make this possible, such as converting a garage or basement, you should do it. The more available personal space there is, the better everyone will feel. Of course, helping with household tasks like cooking, cleaning, laundry, and shopping cannot be taken for granted, and should be discussed, to keep resentment at bay. And then there are guests. Decide with your child on visitor policies that you both can live with. Being honest about your feelings will go a long way toward creating a harmonious time together.

It can be both financially and emotionally challenging to have an adult child move back home. They may need a job, and you may feel that you want to support them. They may be in the process of a divorce, and you feel that you want to protect them and the grandchildren. What makes it extremely difficult is that you need to be concerned about your own finances for the future as well as taking care of them in the present. If the stay is going to be an extended one, it's probably important to talk with your financial planner to determine how much might be realistically available to help them. It also might be important to talk with a therapist to be aware of the challenges of living under the same roof again.

Of course, the ideal situation would be that you have developed a relationship with your adult children that is more like a friendship. Even if you haven't gotten very far with that attempt, there's no time like the present to begin. It's much easier when you can have a conversation as if you were talking with a neighbor, although there may be some rolled eyes and some "oh yeah, Mom," responses now and again. It's up to you to initiate and continue to make the effort to develop this mature adult-to-adult relationship. There are endless opportunities.

SIBLINGS

Another relationship that changes as we age is that with our siblings, who share our family history. It is a time to think back on what it was like to be together when you were younger and to remember the activities that you shared. This time of nostalgia often makes us feel warmth toward one another. As we age, we feel we want to be back in touch. If you have been estranged from your siblings, this is a chance to reach out and reconnect. After all, there's no one else who has known you so long and who shares the same memories.

I think there's so much interest in ancestry and genealogy because we've lost touch with our families. The frequent multi-generational get-togethers that I remember from my youth with grandparents, cousins, aunts, and uncles just don't seem to happen these days. We're all so scattered and busy that it is a big deal to have family gatherings. So we don't hear the stories and know about our ancestors the way we might have fifty years ago. And electronic devices for messaging and email, like the telephone before them, create impermanent communications. Old boxes of letters often told family stories. It's hard to duplicate those in our modern times without a major effort. Writing your family memoir might be a group project that living members can contribute to. Future generations would probably appreciate knowing what went on in your life and the lives of your siblings and other relatives. It doesn't have to be written, but could include videos, audio interviews or reminiscences, or a collage—your imagination and inspiration set the limits.

PARENTS

Living longer has its pluses and minuses. The whole family is affected when a loved one's health declines, she moves to a nursing home, or she moves in with a child. Don't make the mistake of not talking about the changes and hearing the needs of everyone involved. You may decide that having your father move in with the family after his heart attack is a good idea, but he may prefer a move to a retirement community or an assisted-living facility. Most people would prefer to live independently, but a frank discussion of potential problems with all options is essential before making decisions.

Healthy parents may end up moving in with a child in a "granny pod," a converted garage, an addition, or under the same roof. The plus might be that by living together, the family is better able to meet one another's needs for child and elder care. Grandparents may take the grandkids to school and other activities, allowing working parents some flexibility. Cooking, shopping, and other household chores for the extended family may also be a timesaver for the parents. But this has to be agreed to, so the elders don't feel put-upon and come to resent the dependency.

Before setting up an extended household, there should be a task allocation and a financial plan that works for all. If a joint property is purchased or modified, the tax and estate planning consequences for all parties should be taken into consideration. There may be big financial advantages to living under one roof. Money can be pooled for a mortgage or rent, or to offset long-term care expenses. To make it all work, there must be ground rules to ensure privacy and fairness.

Sometimes our elderly parents can frustrate us—as we probably frustrate our children! Repeated stories, forgetfulness, or asking the same question again and again can lead to frustration and annoyance. Put yourself in the shoes of the elder, who probably knows she's not at the top of her game and is also probably scared and saddened by the losses she's experiencing. Maintaining independence is usually at the top of any aging person's list. The best thing you can do is to help make that possible, whether that means leaving notes as reminders, finding out whether the problem is lack of understanding or ability (arthritis can turn something as simple as changing a lightbulb into an impossible task), or redirecting a conversation that's been derailed. Just remember that you were helped with all these issues when you were young and learning to navigate the world. Patience and a sense of humor help.

Of course, caring for parents often requires more interaction among siblings. As parents grow frail, brothers and sisters can often encounter obstacles to togetherness. Sibling rivalry can emerge or intensify as some siblings see one last chance to vie for parental attention or financial gain. At the same time, as parents become more dependent, their desire to remain in charge can lead to family dysfunction and strain. If the children cannot work through their differences, the parents will suffer. And the children will too, once the crisis is over. Working together will preserve the health and sanity of all, according to experts. The best advice: leave the past behind and establish new roles. Bringing up past attitudes ("he can't be counted on") does not encourage an atmosphere that helps anyone. Take steps to share responsibilities and keep everyone accountable. Long-distance tasks can include paying bills, talking with doctors and insurers, finding transportation, and finding paid help. If one child falls into the role of primary caregiver, find ways to support her both physically and financially. Even if she rebuffs offers of help, keep asking. Or seek the help of a friend or other relative to lobby on your behalf. A geriatric care manager, family therapist, or elder mediator might be helpful for those families who can't resolve things themselves. This advice applies to in-laws, too.

FAMILIES BY DESIGN

Not everyone has the luxury or privilege of living near family. That doesn't mean that you can't create your own family with people who are nearby, or, if you're single, you can design your own family from friends, neighbors, their friends, and their children. The options are endless. Most everyone can do with some extra adult attention. Whether that's helping with homework, going on a picnic, spending holidays together, or just making occasional phone calls or emails to stay in touch, these "extra" families can provide all the love, care, and attention that any member of the group needs or wants. And being around people who are younger than you keeps you young and up-to-date with the latest fashions, music, or reading. So don't feel left out if you don't have a family of your own; just create one. After all, we don't generally get to choose our families, just our friends. This way your custom-made family is ideal, since it's made up of friends.

SPOUSE OR PARTNER

"For better or worse, but not for lunch" may be the mantra of women with retired spouses or partners. What to do, now that both of you are at home? Personal space and alone time when you're home together goes a long way toward keeping a relationship on an even keel. It's a shock to no longer be going to work every day, and the adjustment can take some time. If you've lived separate lives with few common interests, it can be especially daunting to get to know one another again and find shared activities to enjoy. When one partner is ill or disabled, the challenges are even greater—but not impossible. Your relationship before retirement can be a guide to how you'll interact as you age. Did you enjoy one another's company at dinner parties? Do you share a taste for sci-fi movies? Did you always want to travel? Start there and build on the commonalities you already know you have. Courtesy and a sense of humor go a long way toward creating healthy relationships, no matter what age. Consider the alternatives: separation or divorce after many years together may be particularly difficult and lead to low self-esteem and pessimism about the future. Changes in lifestyle and finances are the two obvious outcomes of a separation, at any age, but it's still possible to adjust and create a new identity to move forward. Going your separate ways might be the best outcome when you're in a stifling or stunted relationship. At any age, divorce is not an easy decision, but it's one which needs to be honestly and deeply evaluated before acting.

Relationships can be fun, challenging, exciting, boring, and loving. They require constant attention and care. And they can be the most rewarding way to spend our time and energy.

GRANDCHILDREN

Enjoy!!!

~~~~~~

GRANNY BY CHOICE

Do your grandchildren live far away? Do you want to be a "granny" but don't have children or grandchildren? Maybe you'd just like to help a family who could use an extra pair of hands, or be a regular volunteer in a classroom or library, to help with reading skills.

There are organizations like AARP, the American Grandparents Association, or the Facebook group Surrogate Grandparents–USA that can help you get started with finding a match.

What do you want to offer? Shared meals? Child care? Family time together? Outings? Skills like knitting or cooking that you can teach?

Are there social services in the community that know about families in need, or where you can express an interest in helping a family? It could be a religious organization or a group like Kiwanis or Big Brothers Big Sisters of America.

As with finding a job, when you are looking for a family you can help, networking can be an effective tool. Tell people about your desire to be a surrogate grandparent. Before you know it, there will be someone appreciating your time and attention.

8 MAKE NEW FRIENDS, BUT KEEP THE OLD

I only know that in our choice of friends and lovers and
teachers who will change our lives, we are guided by forces
which have nothing to do with the rationalizations we give.
—Erica Jong, *How to Save Your Own Life*

One of the most important aspects of growing older is having a
social network. It can also be one of the most challenging. Current
friends die or move away—or you move. Colleagues from work no
longer have anything in common with you and eventually stop
calling or wanting to meet for lunch. Friends who are couples
seem to disappear if you're newly single—you now only meet for
a "girls" lunch or for dinner when the husband is out of town.
Maybe the tennis group is no longer relevant since you had your
knee replacement. Whatever the reason, we lose friends as the
years pass.

Women are more likely to be alone later in life, so having a
network of friends becomes more essential for them. Not only
increased longevity, but a low likelihood of remarriage, when a
woman is widowed or divorced, add to the importance of friends
for support. Ronan Factora, MD, a specialist at the Cleveland
Clinic Center for Geriatric Medicine, insists that having and maintaining a robust social network is a key feature of aging well (*New
York Times*, March 3, 2011). Why? Social networks offer us people
to talk with to relieve stress. There's a sense of belonging and,
through activities, chances to generate new experiences. There

are opportunities for intimacy and giving and receiving support—emotional as well as physical. Of course, there is also the chance of getting caught up in demanding, negative, or manipulative behaviors from newfound "friends." It is desirable to avoid or dump people like that if necessary.

In many cases our friends become our families. We need more help and support, for good times and bad, which similar-age friends can understand and give. Creating a circle of close friends provides caring and gives meaning to life's experiences. They are the people we can discuss aging and dying with. They offer an easy companionship that allows us to de-stress and fend off loneliness.

But making new friends is not as easy as it once was. If you had children, there was the possibility of meeting people at their schools or activities. Or if you had a job, the workplace provided people to meet and get to know. Now you'll need new strategies for meeting people who could become friends. Adding to the challenge of making new friends—and maintaining old ones—may be poor eyesight or hearing, less energy to pursue sports or activities, maybe even a lack of transportation. It's easy to see how women can become isolated, lonely, and depressed. So let's figure out how to make new friends.

MAKING NEW FRIENDS

The best way to meet new people who might become friends is by engaging in activities you like. If you don't meet anyone you want to spend more time with, at least you've enjoyed the activity. If you're outgoing, being social may be easier for you than for someone who prefers a lot of solitude. The secret is to find activities that suit your temperament and to get involved in those. Regardless of how you interact with the world, chances are good

that you'll have to move out of your comfort zone to meet someone new.

Think about hobbies or interests you've had that were put aside
because work and family required most of your time and energy.
Returning to these may be easier than starting something entirely
new. Take a class or join a group at a church, the library, or a community center. Knitting circles, bingo, and even online groups
can provide new people to meet. Art galleries, yoga studios, and
other specialty shops all give you opportunities to mix and mingle
with like-minded souls. Groups of all sorts—quilting, meditation,
writing, poker, book, investment, travel—are natural starting
points for finding new folks. A website where people with similar
interests can organize focused get-togethers is a good place to
start looking if you're not aware of any groups nearby.

Do you have a dog? Walking a dog always seems to spark conversations, especially at dog parks. Do you sing? Choir practice
or church or community singing groups—gospel, "oldies," folk—
are fabulous places to meet people. Playing music with the town
band can be healthy in many ways. Don't play an instrument?
Drumming circles are everywhere and are easy to join. If you can
count, you'll be a natural. Also, ukulele is easy to learn, and many
ukulele choirs accept members with little or no experience. Check
a music store for all kinds of local music opportunities.

If you're inclined toward learning something new, take a class.
Wine tasting, memoir writing, or social anthropology—anything
you're interested in—can be explored in continuing ed, adult
ed, community ed, or college classrooms, sometimes for free!
And there are numerous organizations that include travel with
study. Road Scholar (formerly Elder Hostel), Overseas Adventures
Travel, and Earthwatch are just a few. Basically, whatever appeals
to you, there's a place to explore it with others who share the
same interest. And if you can't find a group, start one of your own

through your library or senior center, via a posting on a Starbucks bulletin board, or through meetup.com. Just be sure to meet in a public place until you get to know one another.

Anne, seventy-one, knew when she moved to Denver that she'd find a church choir to meet people and make friends. For her, this was a successful strategy that had worked each of the four times she'd relocated. The choir was a place to feel at home and comfortable, even though she was a stranger. It would be a mixed group of people, she knew, but a caring one. The reality of making music together guaranteed a sense of belonging.

Anne's family had moved from New Jersey to Kentucky when she was a senior in high school, the first time she'd been uprooted. Her reaction was to shut down. The family lacked experience in moving, so there were no strategies within the family on how to adjust socially. Instead, Anne focused on her studies, eating alone in the cafeteria and sitting by herself on the school bus. "It was just easier to be lonely," she said. "I was naturally shy, so I just couldn't make the effort needed. I missed the friends I'd known since kindergarten." College was different—everyone was new, and there were planned icebreaker activities for the freshmen. It was at Vanderbilt that Anne first joined a choir, not knowing that it would become her lifelong way of making new friends.

Anne learned from her many moves in her adult life that she needed to make an effort. She forced herself to learn about the possibilities of her new home—museums, parks, neighborhood—rather than dwell on what she'd left behind. Also, to ask for help: "I need a reliable dry cleaner." "What's a good local bank?" The choir was always a resource, so one of the first things she did in her new community was shop for a church. She'd listen to the choir during the service and always stayed for coffee hour afterwards to feel the "vibe."

She suspects that the next move, to assisted living, may be her last, but she'll have the strategies to make the best of that move, too. Her advice: "Be sure to stay in touch with old friends, especially during the transition. Phone calls, email, and Skype keep away the loneliness."

"But I'm not a church person," you say. Maybe Leeann's story will give you inspiration.

Widowhood left sixty-seven-year-old Leeann in a "too-big" house in a neighborhood of couples in Baltimore. She knew after two years that she'd need to move to make a new life for herself. A friend encouraged her to buy a condo in Boston's South End, an area of brick row houses that had been converted to condos over a number of years. She wasn't prepared for the lengthy cold and snow, but discovered an innate sense of survival and self-assurance after the first winter. She knew she could face whatever life threw at her after that!

While her friend provided much of her social life that first winter, inviting her to dinners and asking her to join a book discussion group, Leeann thought spring was a good time to try some things on her own. She saw notices for a volunteer fair to be held at an adult ed center and marked her calendar. She signed up to be a volunteer at New England Baptist Hospital, working in patient care services three afternoons a week, arranging orthopedic care for newly discharged patients. From her fellow volunteers, she learned about her new community and the wide range of activities that were available.

Leeann had been a travel agent, but decided to stop working when she moved. She was ready for a new identity. She joined her neighborhood association and bought a dog for companionship (and to get her out of bed in the morning). She signed up for classes at the adult ed center where she'd attended the volunteer fair. And she got an on-call, part-time job selling fine jewelry at Lord & Taylor department store.

Everywhere she went, she chatted with people—drinking a glass of wine at the bar of a nice restaurant, following up with classmates in her adult ed classes, and with the patients she assisted as a volunteer. She made the effort to be friendly, and it paid off. Within a year she had a group of five friends who decided to travel to London together, and Leeann was happy to make the arrangements. "You have to stay positive and be willing to try things," she advises. "Don't let life pass you by."

All right, you now have some ideas for how to meet people. The bigger challenge is how to move from being simple acquaintances to becoming close friends. We all are surrounded by circles of people:

Acquaintances (any number)—friends of friends, met at meetings or social gatherings, recognized at chance meeting

Friends (four to six)—people you enjoy seeing; friends of good friends

Good friends (three to four)—people you see, phone, or email at least once or twice a month; you'd notice if regular contact was gone; can be family

Close friends (one to three)—very important people in your life; you talk with or see them daily or weekly, share intimate information and support; you can "be yourself"; they require a commitment of time and energy; they can be family.

Meeting people who have common interests is just the start. Over time you'll explore one another's compatibility: shared values, similar worldviews, a sense of reciprocity and support. In

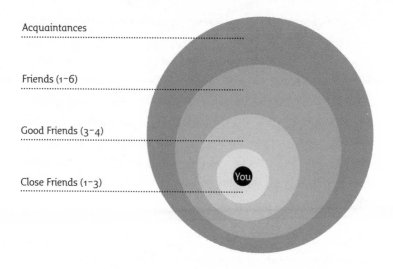

Acquaintances

Friends (1–6)

Good Friends (3–4)

Close Friends (1–3)

You

other words, they're like you in many ways. You may have begun the relationship through shared activities, but involvement with one another based on values means that you're sharing a sense of purpose. Usually not more than one or two friends fulfill these needs. Beyond that are the three to five friends who are important, but less close. They may share your passions—sports, spirituality, art. They are the people you spend time with at activities beyond group events. Some of them may become close friends, but you are happy spending time with them without the need to share your deepest thoughts.

Eva and Luis were snowbirds from Michigan who spent winters in Florida to be near her sister and brother-in-law. In many ways, it was a good decision, but Eva once again felt in the shadow of her sister, as she had when growing up. Luis was happy to play golf every day, and they enjoyed the weekend dinners at the club. But Eva missed having something of her own to focus on.

After a week of watching a trio of women briskly walk past the rental house each morning, Eva went out to ask if she could join them. Of course, they said yes, and she became a regular, chatting with each of the women on various days. They shared basic information—where they had lived, their children's and grandchildren's activities, what they had retired from, what there was to do locally—until they seemed more comfortable sharing political and social views. It was when one of the women mentioned that she was involved with the silent auction for a fundraiser against human trafficking that Eva's ears perked up. She had been involved in fundraising for a residential rehab home for survivors of sex trafficking. She'd heard many stories of survivors in the Hope Project and was happy to find someone who shared her ideals.

Eva invited Janet to lunch, and they chatted about their mutual concern for women forced into prostitution. It was this that allowed the friendship to deepen and continue when Eva and Luis returned north. Eva now considers Janet a good friend. In the summer, the two women keep in touch via Skype and Eva looks forward to their time together in person. And Eva no longer feels in her sister's shadow—she's shining on her own in Florida and Michigan.

Make a friend; develop a friendship. All it takes, sometimes, is the initiative to introduce yourself to a stranger. Maybe we got the wrong message as children—don't talk to strangers. But how else will we meet someone new? Here are some tips for stepping out of your comfort zone to meet people, make friends, and ultimately develop friendships.

MEETING NEW ACQUAINTANCES

Join a group and introduce yourself.

Have a ten- to thirty-second "elevator speech" to use as a summary of what you want people to know about you.

Introduce yourself to new neighbors.

Volunteer.

MAKING A FRIEND

Help acquaintances with information or services.

Join a committee.

Invite acquaintances to activities they might enjoy.

DEVELOPING A FRIENDSHIP

Initiate one-on-one or group activities.

Learn more about your friends' interests and beliefs.

Check in regularly via email or phone, or in person.

Be available to listen.

These are signs of a true friend. Look for these among your current circle and in the prospective friends you're seeking. A friend:

makes time for you

will get you to laugh

will not abuse you—verbally, mentally, physically, monetarily

will defend you if others criticize you

will help you become a better person

To have good friends, be a good friend. But don't get taken advantage of by always being available, or not getting help for yourself when you need it. A few good friends can be enough. And good friends can be of any age, or can be family members.

DATING

Finding a special friend after divorce or widowhood is a different game from when we were young. In addition to friends and family who might be interested in "fixing you up" with someone, there's the whole online dating scene. So many choices. And of course you can meet someone in a class you're taking, on a cruise, at the senior center, at a reunion or even, as Amy did, at a funeral.

Amy's mother, Alice, had always wanted her to date "that nice boy Dave." Wouldn't she be surprised to know they were finally together? And all because of Alice.

Amy was in Seattle for her mother's funeral, having moved to Phoenix in her late twenties with her then husband, Steve. While Amy visited Seattle at least once a year, Alice often preferred to stay in Phoenix where the warm weather was kinder to her arthritis. So Amy's visits to Seattle rarely involved meeting anyone, but rather were quick check-ins. Amy had lost touch with her high school friends, so she was surprised to see several at the funeral, including Dave. They exchanged pleasantries and promised to meet for coffee. But time passed quickly and Amy was headed back to Phoenix, promising her sister she'd return in a few weeks to help deal with Alice's belongings. Dave was there when she got back—and they did make time for coffee. One thing led to another and now they have a regular commuting relationship. Amy hosts Dave in Phoenix where he can maintain his online graphics business, and when she gets a break in her real estate sales, they head off to Las Vegas for some nightlife and a little gambling. The companionship is enough for these divorced singles. But who knows what's ahead.

It's easier, in some ways, to start dating someone from your past. There's a common history, and if you were attracted once, you can be again. Talk with anyone who's reconnected after a high school or college reunion! Life has usually made all of us more interesting. And we also have shared memories. Even if you don't attend a reunion, Facebook and Google provide opportunities to reconnect through a search. But there are opportunities close to home, too.

Susan and Larry are now married, but Susan was married to John and Larry was married to Marie when they first met. The two couples were members of the same church when they were in their forties with young children. Through the years they shared many activities with each other and with larger groups in church. They finally sat together in the same pew only when the kids were gone and all their old friends had died or moved away. And then John died. Marie and Larry and Susan continued on, although Susan often felt like a fifth wheel. When Marie had a stroke, Larry depended on Susan for support. You can guess what happened when Marie died. After a year of courtship Larry popped the question on Valentine's Day. They married soon after, sold both their houses, and moved into an over-55 community to begin again. At sixty-four and seventy, life started over for both of them and is going strong three years later.

"But I don't know anyone like that," you argue. It doesn't matter. If you want to meet someone for companionship or marriage, there are ways. You just need to be willing to move out of your comfort zone and take the initiative. Ask friends to set you up on blind dates. Or join an activity where potential partners might be found: dance classes, computer workshops, hiking or book clubs, group travel (especially cruises). Of course, the free home improvement classes at Home Depot and Lowe's are a natural place for meeting "handy" partner possibilities. And any sports group, whether bowling or kayaking, is a way to get exercise and shop for a partner at the same time.

Kathy met Chuck at the local charity golf tournament. Even though she doesn't play golf, she assumed there'd be many men involved. After her husband's long struggle with Lou Gehrig's disease, she was ready for some fun. She was in charge of assigning the foursomes the day of the tournament, so she got to "check out" all the participants, especially looking for those men without wedding rings. Since she had everyone's name on the list, she put little marks next to the names of those she wanted to learn more about.

The following week she started contacting the men on her list, inviting them to join her for a drink at a local restaurant. There were six "no's" before Chuck. And they've been an item now for four years. He wants to get married, but she likes the current arrangement just fine. They travel together and spend lots of time with each other. His move to her over-55 community makes the commute a lot shorter. But she likes her own space, and they both have children and grandchildren whom they can see and entertain more easily on their own terms.

And don't underestimate the power of a wedding to bring love into the air for the guests, too.

Julia didn't realize she was looking for a new partner when she met Linda at a wedding. Julia was a friend of the bride, Linda a cousin of the groom. Both women had been out of relationships for over a year and each had decided the single life in her mid-sixties was okay. Then they met at dinner under the fairy lights on the hotel terrace. They continued chatting at the bar until the wee hours of the morning, both knowing they would see more of each other. It wasn't long before the daily phone calls and weekend rendezvous evolved to moving in with each other in a new West Hollywood condo. A year later they were the lucky couple being married—on the same hotel terrace, complete with fairy lights.

But maybe you don't have a cousin to fix you up or a social connection for potential partners. Don't despair. There's online dating these days. And women no longer have to wait to be asked out, as they did in the old days. This is the ideal way to reconnect with an old flame. But just joining a dating website can also be a successful venture. If you take a practical approach and enter the dating scene with realistic expectations, you're likely to succeed. Think of dating as an adventure, an exploration of new people with the assurance of experience and the ability to pick and choose. Stay open-minded and be willing to "look beyond the photo" to find interesting people to spend time with. Scott Valdez, of virtualdatingassistants.com, has the following suggestions:

Check out the profiles on a site before you join.

Write a clear profile—use a recent photo and don't lie about your age. Undoing the lies is a shaky way to begin a relationship.

Keep the first date simple, short, and sweet. If there's chemistry, there's plenty of time for another date.

And while you may not meet your romantic partner, you do have the potential for making new friends.

Of course, as with anything online, there are warnings:

Don't share specific personal information up front. This includes your real name, email, home and work addresses, and phone numbers.

Look for inconsistencies and implausible claims when sharing information, to avoid scams.

Research your prospective date online.

Follow your gut.

Read any warnings and disclaimers on the dating website. They usually give tips to minimize your chances of becoming a victim of fraud, as well as how to create a profile and membership information. Online dating can be a great adventure if you approach it the right way.

SEX(Y) AFTER 60

Do older folks still get it on? The National Council on Aging, Indiana University's Center for Sexual Health, and CDC surveys all report a resounding "yes." There's an ageless need for intimacy, and sex can be part of fulfilling that need. Desire can vary widely—true at all ages—but sexual activity generally declines as we age for a wide range of reasons. It may be that you're not really interested in active sex life, and that's perfectly fine. Or you may be ready to try something new. There are no "shoulds," except to do as you like. You can have intimate relationships with or without sex. It's up to you.

Sex can be an emotional experience. If you're in a long-term loving relationship, you've undoubtedly seen your sex life change over the years. You know how to give one another pleasure and adapt to changes in your and your partner's health and mobility. If you've met someone new, you may worry about your wrinkles, body shape, and getting naked. It's likely your partner has the same anxieties, so try to relax and enjoy the sex.

Beth got new lacy underwear and a sheer nightgown for the first night she spent with Ken. Divorced since her late thirties, at sixty-four she felt like a teenager dating again. And in a way, she was. Life had been so busy raising three daughters as a single mom with a full-time commercial real estate job that she'd hardly dated in the years since her divorce. Of course, she'd gone on dates now and then, but because no one had been that interested in a long-term relationship, she hadn't had sex with any of them. And she didn't have "friends with benefits." So when the relationship with Ken evolved over time, of course sex would enter into the equation. And she was nervous. Would she have trouble getting aroused? Did she need lubrication since she'd reached menopause? And what about her body? She was used to seeing the extra inches around her hips and thighs, but she hoped Ken wouldn't want the lights on. Like an actress before the curtain rises, Beth was nervous to the point of feeling a little nauseated, but she didn't let on. What she hadn't counted on was Ken's nervousness, too. He was flabby around the middle and had survived a mild heart attack, so he, too, was apprehensive about what the evening would be like. Beth admitted she was nervous, and Ken laughed and admitted he was, too. The night was spent with lots of cuddling and mutual masturbation, just what they both needed the first time out. After that, well, they ended up getting married and have been happy together for three years. Neither one talks about their sex life now.

By the time you reach sixty, it's likely you know what you like. This especially holds true for satisfying sex—and you shouldn't be put off from asking for what you want. It takes effort to be sexual, and if you're interested you have to make it a priority, especially if physical limitations are involved. Reduced libido from medications or anxiety about heart health or arthritic joints can be factors in your level of desire. Check with your doctor. There are often solutions, but patients are reluctant or embarrassed to ask about them.

Experience and good communication go a long way in creating satisfying sexual encounters. Sharing your fears and expectations and giving feedback and directions can make intimacy possible. If you'd like to experiment with new positions or new ways of arousal, share your thoughts. Maybe you don't have the energy for sex after dinner. You can suggest another time of day to your partner to make the experience better for you. Lifestyle choices, such as smoking or drinking too much alcohol, can reduce your stamina and desire along with the usual declines due to aging. Stress, diabetes, heart disease, high blood pressure, osteoporosis, arthritis, and incontinence can also affect your physical ability to engage in sex. And many prescription drugs can suppress your sexual interest and performance. Be gentle with yourself. Experiment to find what works. The more you know about what to expect, the less anxious you'll be. And laughter helps, too. Sex should be fun, not a project.

"Outercourse" may become more important than intercourse. Touching, cuddling, kissing and mutual masturbation may be all you want. Simple aids like lubricating jelly or medicines for erectile dysfunction can make intercourse possible, if that's what you desire. As we age it may take more foreplay to stimulate our sexual desires. This is where good communication pays off, especially if your partner is not aware of what you like. And when there's too much of something, whether you like it or not, speak up. Don't be shy or embarrassed, or worry about hurt feelings. Honesty and openness are also parts of an intimate relationship. Be playful. Be tender. Touch one another. Relax and enjoy.

Feeling sexy can be part of your satisfying sex life, too. Even if there's no man or woman in your life, that doesn't mean you aren't sexual. Get dressed up with shiny jewelry and flattering makeup. Be passionate about your life and have some fun. That's sexy. Be energetic—that's sexy, too. Smile and laugh. And wear lacy underwear just for fun!

SEXUALLY TRANSMITTED INFECTIONS

It may surprise you to learn that sexually transmitted infections (STIs) are on the rise for the over-sixty population. Diagnoses of genital herpes, genital warts, chlamydia, syphilis, gonorrhea, and HIV / AIDS have increased more than 35 percent in this population since 2013, according to the CDC. Because immunity lessens and vaginal tissues thin as we age, microbes have a greater chance of causing infections. Many doctors are reluctant to talk with their older patients about STIs.

If you're sexually active, use condoms and learn the symptoms of STIs, so that you can get treatment. Safe sex is important at any age, and it's necessary to understand the risks of unprotected sex even when you're not worried about pregnancy.

9 IF YOU HAVE YOUR HEALTH...

One's aim in life should be to die in good health.
Just like a candle that burns out.
—Jeanne Moreau, *The Guardian*, Oct. 31, 2001

Of course, there are physical changes as we age: hair thins, strength wanes, and sometimes balance is a little wobblier. We may need glasses, cataract removal, dental implants, or new hips and knees. The physical self has changed. That's not to say we're not able to climb mountains, garden all day, or run marathons. It's just that we need to tune in more closely to our physical selves, so that we can keep functioning well for as long as possible.

EXERCISING

The good news is that we have some control over the rate of decline. It doesn't matter if you're sixty or ninety, but you need to start. Mark Lachs, MD, director of Geriatrics at New York Presbyterian Health Care System, recommends daily walking and strength exercises to improve balance and avoid falls, since broken hips are often the primary cause of decline as we age. The secret is to stick with it. Small changes, like walking daily and lifting light weights repeatedly, can bring dramatic improvements in quality of life. Don't be a couch potato, in other words.

It took Judy two hip replacements in six weeks before she got on the exercise bandwagon. Using a walker during her recuperation convinced her that she didn't want that as a permanent lifestyle change at sixty-seven if she could avoid it. During her physical therapy, she noticed marked improvement from the first day, when she could hardly lift her leg a few inches off the bed, to walking without a walker—all achieved by doing a few gentle exercises and walking several times a day. She now attends yoga class once a week and walks around her over-55 community daily, unless it's snowing or icy. In bad weather, she uses the treadmill at the fitness center in the clubhouse. At last report, she was with a tour group scaling the steep steps at Cinque Terre in Italy.

More and more research shows that exercise is important for brain function. This is what really motivates me to have at least a daily walk. I value my brain and hope it's fully functional to the end. John J. Ratey, MD, author of *Spark: The Revolutionary New Science of Exercise and the Brain* (2008), explains that healthy brain function is intimately connected to our cardiovascular and metabolic systems. If there's a failure in these, such as heart disease, diabetes, or high cholesterol, then the likelihood of developing dementia rises significantly. It's the death of brain cells or their declining ability to make connections that leads to memory loss and changes in other brain functions. Keeping a healthy blood flow to the brain, via exercise, provides the necessary ingredients for continued brain function. "Because the aging brain is more vulnerable to damage, anything you do to strengthen it has a more pronounced effect than it would on a young adult . . . Exercise is preventive medicine as well as an antidote" (Ratey, p. 224).

Exercise helps not only physically, but also emotionally. Apathy can become a problem when we no longer have jobs to go to or a sense that we're contributing to something beyond our daily routines. And loneliness can intensify as well. Regular exercise that floods the brain with oxygen and other necessary chemicals can counter depression. Exercising with others can provide social interactions that can lead to new friendships. Setting goals and exercise challenges can also stimulate a sense of well-being. Ratey presents a long list of benefits from exercise beyond improving brain function, and I'm sure most readers already know them. But if you need more convincing, please read his book.

The Surgeon General and other government agencies (CDC, HHS, NIH) recognize these benefits from regular moderate exercise (like gardening, bicycling, dancing, walking briskly, water aerobics, and swimming laps, to name a few):

reduces risk of dying from heart disease

reduces risk of developing diabetes, high blood pressure, cancer

helps reduce high blood pressure in those diagnosed

reduces feelings of anxiety and depression

helps control weight

helps maintain bones, muscles, and joints

promotes psychological well-being

helps older adults become stronger and better able to avoid falling

Exercise includes aerobic activities mentioned above, as well as strength training to keep all major muscle groups—legs, hips, back, chest, abdomen, shoulders, and arms—working properly. This can be accomplished through lifting weights, working with resistance bands, and yoga, for example. It's important to do these exercises properly to avoid strains and pulls. Most senior centers have someone who can show you the proper way to use equipment. Having supervision in yoga classes is extremely important, so that you align properly in the poses. You don't want your exercise to damage muscles, ligaments, or joints! I also like tai chi for balance. There are videos and classes, often at senior centers, to help learn the sequence of motions. And meeting others in class can lead to new friendships. Find an exercise you enjoy, so you'll stick with it. Try several types if you need a change in your routine. Some exercise is better than none, and if you enjoy the class or activity, you're more likely to do it.

One challenge of regular exercise is finding the time. Be proactive and schedule a realistic time that works best to get you moving. I find first thing in the morning or late afternoon works best for me, but you may find late morning or midafternoon is better for your schedule. Make exercise a priority and you'll make the time for it. Classes or buddies can also help keep you motivated. And if you have an injury or health problem, permanent or temporary, be sure you modify your fitness plan accordingly. A physical therapist, doctor, or fitness coach can help design a special regimen.

EATING

Another huge factor for successful aging is diet, of course. None of us can eat the way we did as teens and expect to maintain our weight and avoid the diseases associated with obesity (heart disease, diabetes, some cancers, and lots of back and joint pain) unless we do high-energy exercise or sports daily—and that's still a maybe, especially for the joint pain. So why does diet matter after sixty, besides the above-mentioned conditions? Well, there's the immune system and all the organs: lungs, kidneys, liver, and so on. To stay functioning they all need good nutrition—the right kinds of food and liquids. But you already know that, I realize. What gets harder is giving our bodies what they need to recuperate from stress, disease, and poor eating and exercise habits. Changes in appetite, digestion, and even dental health can have an effect on eating. As can depression, boredom, and memory loss.

When taste buds no longer register the same pleasure from food, eating a varied and healthy diet might seem like a lot of work. Frequent snacking or grazing, especially if you live alone, becomes a habit all too easily. Cheese and crackers with a glass (or two) of red wine was often dinner, before I woke up to the realization that it was up to me to take care of me. Now I keep my diabetes under control with diet, exercise, and enough sleep—without meds. I couldn't live the life I wanted with their side effects, so I became very disciplined about what goes into my mouth and forced myself to walk at least thirty minutes every morning. If the weather doesn't cooperate, I use the video *Walking Off the Pounds* (Gaiam) in my living room. Sure, I indulge in chocolate cake and ice cream for birthday celebrations, and I don't deprive myself of anything; I just eat "treats" rarely and am strict about not eating sugars, starches, or much fruit. I've been doing this for about six years now and hope my body cooperates for twenty more. I'm still overweight according to the charts, but I feel better than I did in my fifties, when I was diagnosed and put on pills.

There are plenty of books and programs for weight loss. Find one that works for you if you need to lose weight. Join a group, if that keeps you on target. Be kind to yourself in the process. I keep wanting to wake up forty pounds lighter, but that weight didn't get there overnight, so it's unrealistic to think it will disappear that quickly. Feeling good is the end goal!

Here are some things to think about regarding your nutrition and eating habits that will help to optimize your health:

Learn what foods are beneficial for your current health status.

Read food labels and understand them.

Try to limit caffeine, sugar, salt, additives, fast food, and junk food. (This is an oxymoron: it can't be food if it's junk!)

See if there are vitamins and other supplements you could be taking to optimize your health, since foods do not contain all the nutrients they once did. (Michael Pollan's books have some good information about food.)

Balance a diet of fresh fruits, vegetables, good fats, and meat, poultry, or fish, along with drinking six to eight glasses of filtered water daily.

Whenever possible, choose foods that are not sprayed with pesticides or other chemicals. (There are lists of "unsafe" fruits and veggies online.)

Figure out why you are over- or undereating—stress, depression, boredom, procrastination, anger, or some other issue that is sabotaging you—and seek support to heal and change these unhealthy behaviors.

Try to eat in a relaxed atmosphere, chewing slowly and savoring your food.

If you have signs of digestive problems (gas, bloating, low energy, aches and pains, heartburn, mood swings, food cravings), talk with a professional about possible food allergies.

Enjoy meals with family and friends whenever possible.

If you have a health condition such as multiple sclerosis, diabetes, hypertension, or allergies, there may be special diets that can help you. And there are several food delivery services (HelloFresh, Blue Apron, Plated) that provide all the ingredients and recipes for a wide variety of meals. Chopped vegetables are available in most grocery stores to make meal prep quicker for home cooks. Do whatever it takes to eat nutritious meals as often as possible—optimally, every day. Your body (and brain) will thank you.

DE-STRESSING

But good health isn't only about diet and exercise. Stress can also play a role. It's been medically proven that many diseases result from extended periods of stress. Stress is often described as feeling overwhelmed, out of control, or excessively worried. Some stress can come from positive events (a birth or a wedding) as well as negative ones. Prolonged stress, regardless of the source, is what causes problems.

Extended chronic stress can be both physically and psychologically harmful. Research has associated long-term stress with heart damage, lowered immunity, and higher levels of anxiety and depression. Managing stress is an important skill at any age. We all have different tolerances for stress, but our everyday lives present many triggers, such as driving in traffic and negative news stories. Making ends meet, caring for others, and illness are also stressors. Your body reacts to stress by releasing adrenaline and cortisol. Adrenaline raises your heart rate and blood pressure and boosts energy to your muscles, so that you can "fight or flee" the danger. Cortisol increases sugar in the blood, enhances your brain activity, and makes available substances to repair tissues. It also suppresses the digestive system. These actions are all essential for combating immediate danger such as an impending car accident or a dog chasing you. But constant low-level stress and excess release of cortisol and other stress hormones puts you at risk for a number of health issues: digestive problems, anxiety, headaches, heart disease, weight gain, sleep problems, depression, and memory and concentration problems. Since we cannot stop the stressors, we need to minimize or eliminate the aggravation of stress: this is stress management. Here are some suggestions for easy changes to lower the stress in your life:

Reduce background noise.

Avoid multitasking.

Vary your daily activities.

Avoid people who cause pressure or conflict.

Sit quietly for ten minutes or more at least once a day.

For a little more challenge:

Become more accepting.

Don't take on too much responsibility.

Enjoy nature every day.

Deal with your negative emotions: anger, fear, anxiety, self-judgment, depression.

Don't gossip.

Try not to complain or criticize.

Be open to new ideas.

Instead of bottling up stress and not talking about it—the usual way many people deal with stress—try doing something physical. Perhaps the best thing you can do is reduce or eliminate stress for yourself and others. In other words, become more self-aware and then work to help others to be less stressed. It's just like the instructions for using emergency oxygen masks on airplanes: take care of yourself first, so you can then help others.

There are a number of changes you can make that can help you manage your stress effectively. The secret, of course, is to make them. Strategies to manage stress include:

establishing a healthy diet

taking regular exercise

getting enough sleep

getting a massage

taking time for hobbies, reading, and listening to music

having a sense of humor

seeking professional counseling when needed

practicing daily relaxation techniques: deep breathing, yoga, meditation

Meditation, a medically proven method for reducing stress, is cost-free. All it requires is a quiet space and some time. Sitting quietly, noticing your breathing, and keeping your mind focused on the present moment—breathing, not worrying or planning—can change your attitude. If you can start by doing this for ten minutes and work up to thirty minutes every day, you will calm yourself and de-stress. Paying attention on purpose, or mindfulness, also slows you down and clears your head. Just notice what's going on while you're walking or gardening. What sensations do you feel in your feet, your back? If you have thoughts, just notice them, don't respond. Prayer, guided imagery, yoga, music, and being in nature can provide the quiet to help de-stress.

If you can, try to relax and refresh yourself every day. Maybe that means listening to music or doing something different in your daily routine, like driving a new route to the store or calling a friend for a quick check-in. And don't underestimate the value of a twenty-minute power nap. Of course, it also helps just to smile.

Whether it's diet, exercise, getting more sleep, or focusing on stress reduction, it's never too late to change habits to improve your health. While it may seem difficult, the secret is to take tiny steps and stick with the changes. Here are some tips to make changes into habits that stick:

Write down the plan.

Notice what triggers your impulses for the habit you want to change (quit smoking, go to bed earlier).

Focus on practicing the replacement habit every time you notice the trigger.

It's easiest if you work on one habit at a time. You can focus and not feel overwhelmed or set up for failure. And start small: don't plan to run a marathon if you're not even walking daily. Even five to ten minutes of exercise is better than none. And when that seems too comfortable, add more time. But don't push yourself to the point of pain, or you might quit. Take it slow and steady, like the tortoise. See if you can stick with your new habit for thirty days or more (sixty would be ideal). And make yourself accountable—to a friend, an online group, or maybe just a chart or calendar with check marks or stars—with a nice reward planned for the end of the challenge. Once you've mastered one habit that improves your lifestyle, move on to another. Your success should make you feel more confident about the possibility of change. Just start.

YOUR MEDICAL MINDSET

But optimum health is not only a do-it-yourself project. We all need health-care services at various times and your health and health-care choices depend on your medical mindset. What's that, you ask? Basically, it's your attitude about healthy habits, doctors, medications, hospitalization—everything related to how you manage your health. John Nelson and Richard Bolles devote chapter 7 in their book *What Color Is Your Parachute? For Retirement* (2nd ed., 2010) to understanding your medical philosophy. I'll try to summarize it here.

We're all somewhere on the medical mindset spectrum from "do nothing" to "complete care." What you think about conventional, complementary/alternative, and integrative care will determine what health options you'll choose—whether it's doctors, medications, or care facilities. Knowing your preferences can streamline your search for a new doctor and help you decide if a treatment is right for you.

Conventional and alternative medical practitioners give advice according to their particular medical standards. Your personal choices may be different, and you might feel stressed when advised to take medications or other therapies that you don't agree with. It's important to know your medical mindset before you get sick, so that you don't simply accept whatever treatment is offered without realizing that you have choices.

Conventional medical care options typically include:

MDs (or DOs), nurse practitioners, and physician assistants to provide care

drugs

surgery

physical or occupational therapies

tests

hospitalization

Complementary or alternative care options might cover:

Ayurveda

chiropractic

biofeedback

botanical oils

Reiki/healing energy

homeopathy

hypnosis and visualization

yoga, chi gong, or tai chi

nutritional supplements

therapeutic massage

acupuncture or acupressure

You should also keep in mind which types of treatment are most appropriate for your various health issues:

Urgent health issues ➡ seek conventional treatment

Chronic health issues ➡ may consider alternatives

In addition to your tendency to prefer conventional or alternative medical care (or a blend), what is your attitude toward medical treatment in general? Do you want high-tech or low-tech services? Will you seek out a medical opinion for every sign of illness, or do you have a wait-and-see attitude? Do you want a pill for everything that ails you, or are you willing to tolerate pain, such as arthritis, or change lifestyle habits to improve your health (for example, strict diet control for diabetes)? You may be leaning toward conventional treatments for some health issues but be open to alternatives for others. Here's a list of some common medical concerns to help you determine where your preferences lie.

CONVENTIONAL	ALTERNATIVE
Focus is on curing disease.	Focus is on maintaining health and balancing body systems.
Diagnostic tests are used to identify medical conditions.	Diagnosis identifies the underlying causes, not just symptoms.
Symptoms should be treated with drugs, radiation, or surgery.	Treatments focus on lifestyle changes, diet, and self-care to support the body's ability to heal. May include acupuncture; yoga; supplements; or chiropractic, Ayurvedic, or Chinese techniques.
Patients follow doctors' orders.	Patient takes responsibility for her health and commits to the time required for prevention and healing of chronic conditions.

Note: Unless an illness is caused by an infection, medication treats the symptoms and is not a cure.

How and when you seek care is also part of your medical mindset. Again, where you fall on the continuum can help you define your personal preferences.

As you can see, there's much to consider. The range can be from denial (no intervention) to hypochondria (every possible treatment as soon as possible). Scientific studies are now being applied to alternative methods of treatment and care. The best of both worlds, often called Integrative Medicine, may be available. This approach promotes the lowest level of intervention that supports the body's own healing. The focus is on health and healing, not the treatment of disease. That translates to healthy aging, perhaps with chronic conditions, while emergency needs are treated conventionally. In other words, acute events (like broken bones and heart attacks) receive immediate intervention and

MORE TREATMENT	LESS TREATMENT
See a doctor as soon as symptoms appear.	Wait to see if symptoms persist.
Specialists are essential.	One doctor treats the whole person, not the parts.
More tests and screenings lead to better diagnoses.	Excessive testing may result in overtreatment.
Every medical condition should be treated with medication and/or therapy.	Negative drug interactions may occur if multiple maladies are treated. Some chronic conditions should be managed by lifestyle changes or pain management programs.

necessary medications, but chronic conditions (such as arthritis and digestive issues) may be treated with alternatives.

There are many ways to be sick. Some folks continue with their lives, minimizing any pain or discomfort. Others ignore their illness and don't get enough care. Some are ashamed by their illness, thinking it is a sign of weakness. And of course there are those who constantly use their energy to complain. Knowing how you react to an illness will help you find *your* best solution for managing illness and infirmity.

FINDING THE RIGHT MEDICAL CARE

All right, you've now identified your medical mindset. How do you go about finding the care you want?

When Sherry's husband died, she decided to move to a small town outside Tulsa to be near her daughter's family. While starting over seemed like a big challenge at age seventy-one, none of the changes were as concerning as finding new doctors. Sherry had severe arthritis and was on blood thinners after suffering a heart attack at age sixty-nine. However, she didn't see herself as limited by her conditions. After all, she'd gone to Peru with her husband a month before he died. They'd climbed ruins and walked around Cuzco, all at altitudes she wasn't used to. No, her concerns were that the medical care would not be the same as what she was used to in Houston.

You may feel the way Sherry does—a little concerned about finding new doctors. Yours may have retired, or you're simply ready for someone younger who knows the latest technology in the field. Or, like Sherry, you may have moved and need to find new doctors in your new location. Whatever the reason, here are some tips for finding new doctors, dentists, chiropractors, and other health-care professionals to meet your needs.

If you've already identified your medical mindset, the next steps should be easier. The most important factor is the doctor-patient fit. What is that? Basically, it's the match between what you want and what the doctor provides. Some people want a good bedside manner, others want straight talk about conditions and treatments, while for some their preferred attitude might be, "Just tell me what I should do; don't give me too many choices." There are options. The goal is to find medical practitioners that meet your needs and that you feel comfortable working with. This includes doctors, dentists, massage therapists, nontraditional medical personnel—really, anyone who's involved with your health, whether it involves preventive care, chronic conditions, or acute events. Self-care is included as well.

Finding Dr. Perfect can be a challenge. You can start by asking family and friends, of course. But they may not know anyone with the same medical needs as yours. You can check online as well. Just start a search using "find a doctor near me" and see who comes up. If you're covered by Medicare, go to medicare.gov/physician to find doctors in your area who accept Medicare patients. If you have health-care coverage through another source, the provider has a list of approved medical personnel. Use the same process for finding chiropractors, nutritionists, Ayurvedic or Chinese practitioners, and whatever other specialists you need to see. You can then do more thorough online searches using the doctor's or specialist's name. Look at their credentials and whether any complaints or lawsuits have been filed against them. Customer satisfaction reports need to be read with caution, as other patients' requirements for a good rating may differ from yours—you may have a different medical mindset. Call and ask if you can schedule a short "meet and greet" appointment to see if a practice is a good fit for your needs and temperament. Once you have your primary care needs met, you can ask for referrals to specialists: ophthalmologists, hearing specialists, cardiologists, and so on.

While there is a specialty for aging—geriatrics—there are few practitioners. You'll have to do some homework to find a physician who is sensitive to the needs of older patients. The best place to find a geriatrician is at an academic medical center—a hospital on or near a medical school campus. Geriatrics is usually a part of internal medicine, so start your search by calling that department. If there's no local medical school, you can contact the nearest one to see if there are any graduate geriatricians in your area. If you're a veteran, the Veterans Health Administration could be a resource. Some are associated with HMOs, and your local hospital may have physicians who specialize in elder care. Be prepared to wait for an appointment, since there are so few geriatricians around. Get on the list anyway.

Once you have your appointment scheduled, you need to prepare. Have a list of questions about your primary health issues and be ready to ask how they would be treated. Dr. Mark Lachs, in his book *Treat Me, Not My Age* (2010), suggests that patients be aware of these patterns with any doctors they're considering. Are the doctors

too informal or intimate in a new relationship (calling you sweetie or hon)?

not focusing on you, especially if someone else is accompanying you to the appointment (talking about you to a third party, no eye contact with you)?

interrupting, especially when you are talking about your complaints?

dismissing your complaints, minimizing them, or suggesting they are part of growing old?

quick to test, refer, or prescribe?

A thorough exam takes time, and many tests are unnecessary. Bodies are whole units, and parceling parts out to many specialists can have consequences.

Once you find a medical practitioner you like, the job isn't done. It's important that all interactions be effective and helpful. Office visits are getting shorter and shorter, so it's important to be organized and efficient. Dr. Lachs offers these suggestions to maximize the value of each appointment:

Talk about your "chief complaint." If you can't list specific symptoms, note what functions are being compromised ("I have trouble raising my arms").

Think about and organize your story (when did this pain start? what makes it worse? better?) and add specific details. Write this down for reference when explaining to the doctor.

Prioritize complaints with a Top 3 list.

Be sure to note major health events since the last visit (other medical appointments, infections, falls, surgeries) as well as life events (divorce, new grandchild, death of a friend).

Have a list of your medications that includes dose and frequency, or take along the meds themselves. If you need refills, note them. Medication interactions can be a serious problem, so be sure to include nonprescription medications as well (daily aspirin, vitamins, any herbal remedies).

Get a specific follow-up plan. This might include blood tests, an MRI, a referral to a specialist, or a new prescription. Be sure you understand what you are supposed to do and what the doctor will do regarding follow-up. Don't walk away until you know the specifics and not just the medical jargon.

Developing a good relationship with your medical practitioners will help you feel comfortable with any health-related issue you face. It's worth the time and effort to find people who make you feel good.

MEDICARE ESSENTIALS

While the future status of Medicare is uncertain, for the moment it is functioning as it has since its inception. Who is covered by Medicare? People sixty-five and older, some people under sixty-five with certain disabilities, anyone with ALS (amyotrophic lateral sclerosis, also called Lou Gehrig's disease), and anyone with end-stage kidney disease or kidney failure requiring dialysis or organ transplant. Generally, if you qualify for Social Security you're eligible for Medicare: you or a spouse paid payroll taxes for ten years or more and you are a legal US citizen. There are some exceptions where participants pay a monthly fee for coverage.

Do you even need Medicare? Maybe not, if you have retiree health benefits from a previous job, current employer, spouse, or Veterans Affairs. Deciding which plan is best, once you agree that Medicare is something you want, can be the next step. There are costs and coverage to consider.

HMOs (health maintenance organizations) have the lowest premiums, but restrict the physicians and hospitals you can choose. Specialist visits require referrals and may need pre-approval. These plans also include prescriptions.

PPOs (preferred provider organizations) have lower premiums than fee-for-service plans and offer out-of-network care without a referral, but at additional cost. Most offer prescription drug plans.

Fee-for-service (FFS) plans are the most expensive, but give the most flexibility in choosing doctors and health-care facilities. They also have the most generous coverage, but that translates into more expensive options.

If you're on a limited income with few assets, you may qualify for financial assistance with premiums, deductibles, and co-pays for prescriptions. The Qualified Medicare Beneficiary (QMB) program is managed by the states. Talk to your state Medicaid office to see if you qualify. You do not have to be on welfare and you must not be eligible for Medicaid. Contact socialsecurity.gov for more information.

What is covered by Medicare? Medicare Part A covers inpatient hospitalization, temporary nursing home stays, hospice, and home health services. Medicare Part B covers basic medical services (lab tests, doctor visits, surgeries, ambulance), medical supplies (wheelchairs, walkers), preventive health services, and mental health care. Everyone on Medicare gets these services. Confusion can arise about Medicare Parts C and D.

Medicare Part C is called Medicare Advantage. These are plans which include parts A and B plus prescription drugs (Medicare Part D) and vision plans or dental plans at an additional fee. Medicare Advantage Plans include HMOs, PPOs, and Medicare Medical Savings Account plans.

Medicare Part D encompasses prescription drug plans and must be signed up for at the same time as enrolling in Medicare A and B. This might be a good option if you still are covered by an employer's health plan that doesn't include prescription drugs.

There are other Medicare plans, like PACE, the Program of All-Inclusive Care for the Elderly. Then there are Medigap supplements—private plans that cover out-of-pocket expenses not covered in the basic plans (for example, deductibles and co-pays). The National Committee for Quality Assurance (NCQA) has an annual ranking of Medicare Advantage HMO plans. You may want to check the list at ncqa.org before you choose a plan.

Obviously, the best source for up-to-date information is at medicare.gov. You can also enroll on the site.

MEDICARE DOS AND DON'TS

Medicare enrollment can seem complicated, the following suggestions can help:

DO sign up for Medicare ahead of your sixty-fifth birthday if you want coverage to start then. The regular enrollment period runs from three months before until three months after your birthday. If you sign up later, you will be penalized for the duration of coverage. The exception is if you retire from an employer with twenty or more employees. Then you have three months to enroll without incurring a penalty. If you're still working and have health benefits, you need to sign up for Medicare Part A, which covers hospitalization. If the business employs twenty or fewer employees, you should also sign up for Part B. Even if you choose not to enroll in Part B, you can enroll in Part D, the prescription plan. If you're covered by an employer's plan, you should receive a letter from the insurer that indicates that your coverage is "creditable." If not, you should enroll in Part D, or again, a penalty will be imposed if you sign up later. If you currently receive Social Security benefits, you will be automatically enrolled in Medicare Parts A and B effective the month you turn sixty-five.

DO choose a plan that considers your needs: doctors, medications, co-pays, and any extras you want (like eye exams and dental care).

DO evaluate whether you need a Medigap Supplement or the Medicare Advantage Plan.

DO remember that different rules apply to each part of Medicare. Be sure to check the information you receive to see limits on care, length of hospital stay that's covered, and which pricing tier your drugs are on.

DO review your plan during the annual enrollment period to see if it's still the best choice for your needs.

DON'T confuse Medicare Advantage with original Medicare. They have different rules and choices of coverage and care.

DON'T be hospitalized for "observation" if you can help it. This is considered an outpatient service by Medicare. This means higher out-of-pocket expenses and fewer Medicare benefits. The general guideline for admittance is two over-nights. If a stay is shorter, the designation is "observation." Ask to be admitted. Observation patients cannot receive Medicare coverage for follow-up nursing home care, as the requirement for coverage is three consecutive days as an ad-mitted patient, not including the day of discharge. Check your status daily. It could change from "admitted" to "observa-tion," with the attendant increased costs. If you've been under observation and then need rehab, ask for home services that should be covered by Medicare Home Health Care benefit. You can appeal any rehab facility charges according to your Medicare Summary Notice, issued quarterly.

DON'T get caught in a Medicare scam. If anyone contacts you to enroll you in Medicare, it's a scam. You need to sign up in person at a Social Security office or online at medicare. gov. The government contacts you by mail, not by phone or email. Beware of anyone who contacts you by phone or email, especially anyone asking for personal information and a So-cial Security number.

While there's a lot to think about when choosing a Medicare plan, there is help available. Take advantage of free help to an-swer your questions. You can get one-on-one assistance from your State Health Insurance Assistance Program (SHIP). Many counselors are available at senior centers. Go to shiptalk.org to find the contact in your state. SHIP counselors work with you to determine the best plans based on your medical and prescription needs. It is well worth a visit. Just a note: the SHIP program in your state may have another name. For instance, Massachusetts and Florida call their programs SHINE (Serving the Health Insurance Needs of Everyone).

PUBLIC POLICY AND HEALTH CARE

Public policy emphasis is on services that replace family, rather than services that support family caregiving (like nursing homes rather than home care). Public policy has traditionally viewed informal caregivers' service as a personal, moral obligation, and not as an extension of the workforce, even though they play a substantial, but often underappreciated, role in the health-care delivery process. Their roles will be even more substantial in the future, given the rising incidence of chronic disease, which requires greater self-monitoring on the part of patients, and the rapidly increasing number of older Americans, which will place greater responsibilities on family and friends to provide care assistance. Recent NIH studies indicate that taking on the role of informal caregiver increases the risk of elevated stress hormones, physical illness, psychological distress, and mortality. Approximately 80 percent of adults requiring care live at home and get help primarily from unpaid family and friends ("Rising Demands for Long-Term Services and Support for Elderly People," Congressional Budget Office Report, 2013).

10 BRAIN GYM

I am learning all the time. The tombstone will be my diploma.
—Eartha Kitt

"Use it or lose it" applies particularly to brain function. Learning new things, whether in the context of formal classes or experiencing new events, is the perfect means to keep the gray matter healthy. Tasks as simple as brushing your teeth with the non-preferred hand or driving a new route on the way to the grocery store will keep the brain active. Of course, eating well and taking regular exercise will get all the nutrients to those brain cells and keep them healthy.

The jury is still out on whether or not brain exercises such as brain teaser games or puzzles can slow the decline in brain function. But if you enjoy doing crosswords, sudoku, jigsaw puzzles, or any other brain games, keep doing them. It's important to challenge your brain, so if you are a lifelong crossword puzzle person you might want to try something new. Something that's novel and challenging is what strengthens memory. Word games, strategy and memory games, bridge, mahjongg, or chess. This may be the perfect time to try something that you've always wanted to do. Maybe it's playing a musical instrument, learning a new language, or taking up painting. It's not too late. It's also important to stay socially active and be as happy as possible. The more brain interactions that occur, the more likely you are to stay brain healthy. While it was once concluded that brain cells do not regenerate, there's new evidence that this is not true. We're forming new brain cells all the time, as long as there is new stimulation. And new stimulation doesn't have to be exotic or expensive. Writing your thoughts in a journal every day, participating in a book discussion group, or enjoying a nature walk and making new observations will help in making new brain connections.

One of the more exciting developments of the last two to three decades is the rise of lifelong learning programs associated with colleges and universities. These are somewhat formal programs where participants decide the topics they want to teach and students choose the subjects they want to attend, so there's a lot of participation on everyone's part. This is a chance to study something new, such as the history of cheese, animals in pre-Columbian North America, or radio programs before 1950. Obviously, the topics are wide-ranging to meet the needs of the instructors as well as the students. They aren't necessarily "academic," as you can tell from the "history of cheese" topic: these were all course offerings at a lifelong learning institute that I recently attended. There's a national organization called the Osher Lifelong Learning Institutes which provides access to information about local programs if you're not aware of any near you.

But you don't need a formal program to pursue lifelong learning. Here are some ideas of things to try on your own:

Look up a new word every day and try to use it three times.

Listen to audiobooks or language CDs or mp3s while you drive.

Write a letter to the editor of a newspaper or magazine sharing your opinion on something.

Sign up for a course, workshop, or seminar on a topic of interest, or go to a lecture.

Make a list of books to read for the next year.

Visit a museum or gallery, maybe of an art type you're not familiar with or don't like.

Try a media-free weekend: no TV, books, magazines, email—nothing but your own thoughts.

What about renting out your house and taking to the open road or starting a grand tour of Europe? Or consider a house swap. What a great way to spend time visiting a foreign country and learning all about it. That's a great brain stimulus. Try a home exchange, if this is a possible option for you. There are also teaching opportunities around the world where classes in English are in high demand. Spending extended periods of time in another culture deepens understanding and stimulates your brain at the same time. What could be better?

Of course, not everyone can leave home. But that doesn't mean you need to be less stimulated and restricted in your opportunities. The Virtual Senior Center operated by Selfhelp Community Services allows you to get involved in intellectual and cultural events online. There are courses as diverse as tai chi, gallery talks, and music appreciation. And it'll allow you to try many new things, even piano lessons. Swipe the "hello" button on a touchscreen computer to get fully involved.

Along with lifelong learning courses at colleges and universities, there are specialized programs, such as Road Scholar (formerly Elderhostel), which combines travel and learning for people over fifty. Voluntourism offers a wide range of possibilities. There are projects in sustainable development through Projects Abroad that might interest you. Broadway Fantasy Camp offers short-term one- to five-day musical theater camps. If you've always wanted to act, this may be your chance. Is the next great American novel inside your head waiting to be written? There are writers' camps and conferences across the country. Why not combine a vacation with a writing conference in some romantic locale? Or maybe you want to let your inner artist out. Haystack, Penland School of Crafts, Shenandoah Art Destination, Snow Farm, Thousand Islands Art Center, and Idyllwild Arts are just a few of the many residential options possible for pursuing art of all kinds: painting, weaving, sculpture, metalwork, glass, mosaics, photography, quilting, or woodworking. Do some online searching to find something that's near you, or take an art vacation.

Adventure vacations are also exciting ways to learn new things. The Culinary Institute of America has a boot camp. Learn to cook like a master chef. If winemaking is more your interest, Cornell University has a viticulture and enology experience. Or join a museum trip that explores archaeological digs where you can get your hands dirty. And the Peace Corps doesn't have an age limit. For more information, check with a recruiter.

Theater is a fabulous way to develop social connections and keep your brain active. Classes in standup comedy and improv are great ways to keep your brain limber. You have to listen, you have to be quick on your feet, and you have to pay attention to what the audience and your fellow actors are doing. You may even get the production bug, whether it's directing, handling the lights, or actually writing a play.

Laurie's move to an over-55 community was quite a shock after living in a neighborhood with children as well as active adults. She was having trouble connecting with the senior residents. One morning soon after she moved in, she accidentally locked herself out when she let the dog out. She thought she could get back in through her garage, but couldn't remember the code to open the door. Of course, she was in her pajamas and it was only 6:15. She noticed a light on in the living room of the house across the street and decided to knock on the door. She wasn't sure what help she would find, but didn't want to stand outside in the chilled morning air. An unshaven, gray-haired, paunchy man looked suspiciously through the open curtain of the front window. Laurie waved to him and smiled, hoping to convince him to open the door. Instead his wife appeared on the other side of the storm door, opening it slightly to ask what was the matter. Laurie explained her dilemma and was invited in, along with her dog. A quick call to the management company brought a locksmith who solved the problem.

Laurie decided to write about the incident, and it became the basis for a short one-act play. Laurie had trained as a graphic designer, and writing a play was a whole new experience for her. She knew there was a small acting group within the retirement community and went to them for guidance. The eighty-year-old woman who was the director of most of the plays accepted Laurie's play as a new project. After several months and some contentious rehearsals, Laurie's play was performed. There was lots of laughter, and that was all the reward Laurie needed to start work on another script. She'd caught the bug.

Have you always wanted to play a musical instrument? Why not start now? There are some challenges to picking up an instrument when you're old, including coordination, memory, and eyesight concerns. But there is an upside. Adults have better motivation and better focus and are better at picking up concepts and drawing on life experiences to help their learning. You can either practice playing in the privacy of your own home or join others to play in small groups, at recitals, or even at the town bandstand. Is rock 'n' roll more your style? Get an electric guitar or a set of drums and start jamming. You can put together a group that will be the hit of the senior center! It's easy to get started. Just rent an instrument and find a teacher via an online search. That's how my brother started playing the tenor sax, my sister the flute, and I the Celtic harp. Maybe someday we'll all play together!

Is there some project you have a yearning to complete? Now may be the time to get started. Make your dream a reality.

Annette, single, never married, had always worked in community organizations, first as a Peace Corps volunteer and administrator, then in her hometown as the school-community liaison, and later as a community health advocate against tobacco products. When she turned sixty-one, however, she knew she was ready to pursue her true love: writing. After recovering from injuries sustained in a serious automobile accident, she had a sense of urgency about doing something personally important. She decided to write a script for a documentary on smoking and air pollution in the third world, places where education about the dangers of smoking isn't as advanced as it might be. Her goal was to find a video-maker or filmmaker who would hire her for this project. She knew she could not completely quit her day job, so she reviewed her finances and decided she could manage for about six months if she cut back her work schedule to three days a week while working on the project. She borrowed money from friends to buy a new computer and started writing the outline and proposal to present to potential filmmakers. She woke up at five o'clock each morning to write for two hours, then either went to her office or made phone calls to network with people she thought might be interested in her project. After four months, a film professor at a nearby university agreed to take on her project if she would help write the funding grant. Although her time and money were running out, Annette helped write a grant that won funding, and began working in earnest on the script nine months after she had decided she wanted to pursue this new focus. She was thrilled to finally be using her energy to do what she wanted.

Whatever it is that you want to do, move beyond thinking to acting. Now is the perfect time to try something new to keep your brain functioning at its optimum. Find help if you need it. Take your talents and follow your interests to discover a new sense of purpose and usefulness. Lifelong learning is just that—something you do your whole life. You don't have to look any further than your own imagination and your lifetime of dreams to decide what you want to do.

WHY LIFELONG LEARNING?

According to the Pew Research Center, adults seek additional education for a variety of reasons. Here are a few:

to pursue knowledge in an area of personal interest, to make life fuller and more interesting

to help others more effectively

to turn a hobby into something that generates income

to learn things that would help keep up with the schoolwork of their grandchildren or other kids in their lives

to maintain or improve job skills

to feel more capable and well rounded

to get new perspectives on life

to make new friends

to feel more connected to the local community

to get more involved in volunteer opportunities

Courses are usually available locally, but there are also opportunities for the use of the Internet for learning through massive open online courses (MOOCs) offered by universities and companies.

Whatever you want to learn, there's someone teaching it!

# WE'RE IN THIS TOGETHER

I also believe that it's almost impossible for people to change alone. We need to join with others who will push us in our thinking and challenge us to do things we didn't believe ourselves capable of.

—Frances Moore Lappé, *Mother Earth News*, March/April 1982

Being involved in community has been heralded as an important element of healthy aging. A community can be a place to give back, for you to help others while enhancing the community as a whole. You're already a member of many communities, even if you're an introvert and believe that you live an isolated and solitary kind of life. Just think about it for a minute: you're part of a neighborhood no matter where you live—in a high-rise, assisted-living facility, or your own home. If you visit the library or the post office, you're interacting with the larger community, one that's part of a local, state, or national group. There are all types of communities, with many opportunities to get involved. Here are some possible ideas for the groups that you are already participating in. Think about what you give to your communities and what you get from being involved. Add to the list with your own unique communities.

Neighborhood—safety, education, beautification

Town or city—library, senior center, housing

Political—local, state, national, international

Regional—transportation, watershed, air quality

Family—immediate and extended, including created family

Business or workplace—current or former

Worship or meditation—formal or informal

Health—special program for diet, heart, or cancer

Exercise—gym, health club, golf, tennis

Music—band, singing, drumming

Civic organizations—Kiwanis, Rotary, others

Learning—adult education, college, other schools

Women's group—formal or informal

Hobbies—knitting, sewing, scrapbooking

Leisure—playing bridge, book group

You might be volunteering your time and expertise, or you may just participate as a member of a social group. No matter where your participation falls on that spectrum, you can contribute something and affect someone. Sometimes just listening is enough.

Do you participate in community theater, choir, band, or orchestra? Your performance can bring smiles to the faces of your audiences. Are you near a museum, historical site, national park, or national monument? As a guide, you can enlighten others and learn a few things yourself. There are food pantries and meal programs that can always use helping hands. Libraries often provide books to shut-ins who truly appreciate when a volunteer makes a delivery visit. All of these activities contribute to a healthy community.

Maybe you'd like to be an usher at local cultural events, read for the blind, or sponsor an international student to acquaint them with local attractions. You can volunteer for a blood drive, answer phones for public television pledge drives, or use your business skills with the local chamber of commerce. You don't need special skills for many of these activities.

Is there a cause you believe in? You can help with fieldwork or outreach. Do you have gardening skills? Beautification projects are probably looking for help to plant and weed. Read to young children at the library or volunteer in the schools. Extra hands and hearts are always welcome. There's no dearth of projects out there. There are so many issues that need attention. And there are many political and social issues that directly affect women where your support is in demand.

The following issues are particularly important to the community of older women. Even if you're not interested in becoming involved in raising awareness or making changes, it's helpful to know as much as possible about the issues.

MEDICARE

The most obvious health issue is the future of Medicare. Since women live longer, on average, than men, medical expenses are likely to be an issue over time. The costs of prescriptions and availability of care for geriatric patients are topics which can use investigation and support. Payment for services, especially support for family caretakers, needs reassessment as well. Currently payment goes to institutions such as hospitals, nursing homes, and home care service companies, not to individuals. Yet there are not enough nursing homes to provide care for the expected population, and today most care for the elderly is done by family members, especially spouses or partners. People will need to get involved and push for change if they expect other options to become available.

Joanie has been taking care of her mother for more than ten years, something she did not expect. She moved back "home" when her mother was ninety-one and no longer able to drive. At the time, Joanie was divorced and her own children were out of the house. The youngest of three siblings, she had the most flexibility. It seemed logical that she would be the one to disrupt her life as an insurance broker in Detroit and move back to Milwaukee. So she took early retirement and rented her house to make the move.

Her siblings visit for two or three days every so often to give her a break, but Joanie is the primary caretaker for a nonagenarian who can't quite manage living on her own anymore. At first, her mother was able to dress herself, but with her failing eyesight she couldn't always match colors or the designs of blouses and skirts. Her hearing aids were a big help, when she wore them, but if they started whining she took them out. And then the shouting began.

Now 101, Joanie's mother is not quite able to manage any of the daily routines by herself—dressing, toileting, eating—and relies on Joanie's help all day and sometimes during the night. She naps during the day in a recliner in the living room, which gives Joanie a break. When Joanie's mother could no longer manage stairs, a hospital bed was set up in the dining room. Nearly blind and deaf, she bemoans the fact that she's lived so long. Her friends are all dead and her children, grandchildren, and great grandchildren only visit occasionally. And she doesn't leave the house anymore. It's a challenge for Joanie, too. She tried putting her mother in a nursing home, but after only a week the experiment came to an end. Joanie's mother missed the familiarity of her home of over sixty-five years and didn't like being "parked" in front of the TV in the common room for most of the day. Currently a nurse visits Joanie's mother at home for bathing and general checkups, but otherwise Joanie is on her own. She's had to use money from her mother's account to pay the bills, buy groceries, and fill prescriptions. She suspects her siblings are upset that she's spending their inheritances, but she gets no compensation for the time and care she's giving her mother, and she feels she's due something for the investment and radical change of lifestyle. Joanie could not have predicted that she would spend ten years as caretaker, and she wonders how much longer she'll be needed.

And Joanie's not alone. Eighty percent of centenarians are women, many of whom are under the care of family members (US Census, 2010). If women leave jobs to take care of family members, it's impossible to make up lost salaries and retirement benefits. Finding a new job after an extended period of not working can also be an almost insurmountable challenge for the caretaker who's in her sixties. State and federal health policies have not been updated to the realities of our current health needs, and all women should be concerned that these caretakers not be left without resources both during the caretaking years and afterward. This could be a cause that you take up and work for: learn what policies need to change and help make the necessary changes a reality.

SOCIAL SECURITY

Income inequality, time off for child-rearing or family caregiving, and longer lifespans all present challenges for those living on Social Security payments, even if they're not the sole source of income. According to an August 12, 2016, website update, the nonpartisan Center on Budget and Policy Priorities reported: "For 61 percent of elderly beneficiaries, Social Security provides the majority of their cash income. For 33 percent of them, it provides 90 percent or more of their income. Reliance on Social Security increases with age, as older people—especially older women— outlive their spouses and savings. Among those aged 80 or older,

Social Security provides the majority of income for 72 percent of beneficiaries and nearly all of the income for 42 percent of beneficiaries."

Changes to Social Security have a disproportionate impact on women. Even elimination of the cost-of-living increase can have devastating effects in the face of continued increases in prescription, food, and gasoline prices. And there doesn't seem to be much relief in sight. If anything, cuts and limitations on eligibility seem to be on the horizon. The safety net is sagging and could collapse entirely. Everyone should be involved in improving this situation, not just older women. But we have the most at stake in the outcome, so this is an issue where getting involved helps everyone, especially yourself.

TRANSPORTATION

Can you get to where you want to go on public transportation? Is there a bus that can take you to the doctor or the dentist? What about religious services on Saturdays or Sundays? In so many places, both urban and rural, public transportation leaves much to be desired. Whether local or regional, bus, train, and special-needs transportation services generally do not have the funding or personnel to be adequate for the needs of the community. There may be an easy fix, such as a local community purchase of a minibus to service the senior center by making trips to grocery stores, doctors, and the post office.

Transportation issues are not only elder issues. Students, young mothers with children in tow, and anyone trying to get to work in a less polluting way are also dependent on buses, trains, or carpools. Isolation is damaging to mental health, especially in older women. Being able to get around and go where you want, when you want, requires a community-based solution. But these services require advocacy and coordination with local or regional governments. This could be your chance to find out what you can do to make it possible.

HOUSING

Whether you're living in your own home, in an apartment, or with roommates or family, housing is an important and costly part of your happiness and survival. Many housing options need to be made available to meet the needs of elderly residents, whether it's a new multifamily design, cooperative housing in which multiple generations interact, or just single-family homes with modifications.

Sidewalks that are safe and not buckled by tree roots or uneven pavements are the responsibility of the larger municipality that the neighborhood is a part of. Are the streets safe? Is there adequate lighting? Do police and emergency services arrive in a timely fashion? All of these are concerns for elderly residents—and really, they're concerns for everyone in the neighborhood. In order for a neighborhood to remain vital, residents must feel safe. Work with your city or town officials to make the changes that are necessary. Maybe even run for office yourself. Safe communities are good for everyone, not just the older residents.

ACCESSIBILITY

We normally think of accessibility issues as a concern for handicapped people, particularly those in wheelchairs. But an aging population also may have needs for adjusted mobility and accessibility. People with arthritis, those using walkers, and those with an unsteady gait are more common than people in wheelchairs, and they have a need for the same accommodations that wheelchairs require. For instance, bathrooms that are considered handicapped accessible are often really just "handicapped available." Entry doors are often heavy, and the handicapped stalls are frequently at the back of the room rather than near the door. All bathrooms could benefit from easier access, higher toilet seats and handrails, and more of the accessible stalls. These are simple changes, but someone has to think of them and advocate for them. Getting involved with efforts to improve compliance with the Americans with Disabilities Act is one way you can participate, whether you need accessible facilities or not.

ENVIRONMENT

Clean air and clean water are important for everyone. We all need to advocate for municipal services that keep our water clean and work to limit air pollution wherever possible. We've lived long enough to remember what it was like when our cities were covered in smog. I grew up in Cleveland and can recall when the Cuyahoga River caught fire due to toxic paint product discharge. We all deserve a better environment for ourselves and for future generations. You can easily get involved with planting trees in your community, as well as protesting "dirty" businesses that pollute the air, the ground, and the water. It doesn't take much to protest by writing a letter to the newspaper, attending a town meeting, or speaking to your representatives in the state or federal legislatures. A few phone calls is all it takes to get involved.

CLOTHING DESIGN

Do you often feel frustrated when shopping for new clothes? I know I do. The latest fashions don't really seem to take into account arthritic joints, with fingers that limit buttoning or arms you can barely raise over your head. Who wants underwear that hooks in back when your arms don't bend that way anymore? Or shoes that are neither safe nor comfortable, let alone stylish? Although many clothing designers are themselves in our age demographic, they seem to design only for young, thin women, not the mature, fuller body with a few limitations in movement. I prefer blouses with sleeves that come to either the elbow or the wrist, but often find only sleeveless or three-quarter-length sleeves that are not warm enough in the winter. I also like solid-color shirts, tops, and pants, but can only find large flower prints or horizontal stripes. I'm not sure what we can do to get clothes designed for us—women of a certain age who have style and want to feel comfortable. But maybe you could take a page from Iris Apfel's book— she's over ninety and wears whatever suits her fancy! Millions of older women would be grateful if someone designed for us.

As a member of many communities, especially the community of women, it's possible for you to effect change yourself, or else support measures that serve communities of all ages. Important changes meant to accommodate us older folks will often go far to serve others as well. This is a golden opportunity to get involved and make durable change to make our lives better. Please do what you can.

GET INVOLVED

Learn who your elected officials—local, state, and federal—are at usa.gov.

Attend town hall meetings.

Support organizations that are already doing the work you're interested in.

Speak up about issues that matter to you.

Run for office.

12 LIFE'S LEFTOVERS
YOUR LEGACY

What you leave behind is not what is engraved on stone monuments,
but what is woven into the lives of others.
—Thucydides, *History of the Peloponnesian War*

Like the remains of a delicious meal, what you leave behind from
a life well-lived can feed others. It's possible to make conscious
decisions about what a legacy will be. It can encompass financial
contributions, of course, but also less tangible elements—lessons
for living. You want to be remembered for what you contributed
to the world. That may be something monumental—like the solution for global warming. Or more modest—a favorite family recipe
for chocolate chip cookies. If you've made a difference in the lives
of others, then you've left the world a better place. Our legacies
are as much about sharing who we are and what we believe as the
financial resources and belongings we leave behind.

TELLING YOUR STORY

When you are gone, no one will know your stories—unless you
share them. In today's busy world where families are scattered
and communities grow beyond the point of knowing everyone
in town, it's important to somehow record your memories and
achievements. This record may be written. It may include photos
and videos. It may be voice recordings or a scrapbook. You choose
whatever method you want. The important thing is to record your
life story. Before you begin, ask yourself these questions. Who am

I telling my story to? Family and friends? Business associates? Community archives? Do I want to tell the story of my whole life or only specific events? They may lead you to choose one format over another.

If you decide to write your story down, there are many forms from which to choose. A diary or journal is the least formal. Dated entries in a journal capture the emotions of the moment or offer insights into what happened on that day, while a diary records the details of an event. Memoirs are vignettes of life events that may or may not be in chronological order. The events somehow affected you, or they wouldn't remain in your memory. An autobiography generally tells the full story of a life and is typically in chronological order. There are many examples of memoirs and autobiographies in libraries and bookstores if you need them. Natalie Goldberg's 2002 book, *Old Friend from Far Away: The Practice of Writing Memoir*, offers great prompts to get you started if you have trouble on your own.

But don't feel constrained by writing. Creating a scrapbook using photos, newspaper clippings, old letters and cards, and favors from dances or parties can be just as important. This is your story, and whatever helps you to tell it should be included. Maybe even some of the music you listened to. If you're not a writer, a voice recording on your computer or phone, with or without video, can be a great record of your story.

This isn't usually a one-time project. What often happens is that the retelling of one event reminds you of others, and then before you know it, you're tired and need to put the project aside for another day. You may need to check with others for some of the details of an event. Or maybe you'd like to put it into the broader context of what was going on in the world or in your family or community at the time. You may need to do a little research to flesh out the details. This might now seem like a huge project, but it's like eating an elephant—you do it one bite at a time. You just have to start. It doesn't matter how long it takes to finish. Remember, no one else can tell your story.

Olga and her husband, Jura, escaped Czechoslovakia after the Soviet invasion in 1968. They left parents and a younger sister behind, fearing as they headed to Toronto that they would never see them again. But in 1990 the regime had changed and they were able to visit. By then Olga and Jura had become Canadian citizens and had raised two teenagers. Olga's parents were both in poor health, and she was glad they could see one another one last time. Jura's mother was widowed and very glad to see Jura reunited with his sister and her family. The visit was filled with meals shared with neighbors and extended family, as well as trips to sites that had played a part in Olga and Jura's youth, including the college campus where they'd met. However, much had deteriorated under Soviet rule, and both were saddened by the decline.

Jura died in a car accident in late 2012. By that time Tina, their daughter, was a mother herself for the second time. And Jakob, their son, had been transferred to the London office of Royal Bank with his family. Olga, now a retired dental hygienist, decided to spend some time writing about her life in Czechoslovakia, the challenges of being an immigrant, and why the traditions she maintained at the holidays were so important. As an only child, she was the only one who could tell the story of her family. She is excited about becoming an author and plans to have copies printed and bound by a local copy shop for the grandchildren.

If you want to share your own story, but maybe don't know where to start, here are a few questions to ask that can get you started:

Where am I from? Who are my people?

What have been my life-defining events? Marriage, birth of a child, dream job . . .

What have been my most important roles in my family? In my community? What was my most important job?

What are my most important accomplishments?

What are my regrets? Is it possible to change any of them?

Have fun walking down memory lane as you tell your story.

SHARING YOUR VALUES

The facts and details of your life are generally easy to share. But sharing what you believe in and showing how you lived those ideals can be a little trickier. First, you need to look at your own life and identify the values that mean something to you and how you lived them—or the regret when you didn't. Was friendship important? If so, how were you a friend? Were you a leader? If so, why was that important and what was your leadership style? Did you transform your life? Inspire others? Make beautiful art to share? Did you have and follow a purpose?

What about honesty? Trustworthiness? Faith? Find examples of how these played out in your life and share them. Love of family? Hard work? If these are values you want to instill, you've probably lived your life as an example. Think of some specific stories that highlight or reveal their importance. Did you support a political cause? Explain why that was important. Maybe you think a sense of humor is essential. How has it worked in your life? Is the natural environment something you treasure? Do you share your love of the outdoors with family and friends? Think about how those shared experiences will linger after you're gone. Maybe it's just being a good listener that matters.

How do you feel about work? What was your first job like? Did you learn about money—and about spending it? What are your special gifts? How did you use them? What can you pass on about following your dreams? How did you make the world a better place? There's so much to convey.

You can share your values in letters, face-to-face conversations, or as a collage, quilt, video, scrapbook, or other art medium. Sometimes this is referred to as an ethical will and can be included with your traditional will. If you want help getting started, personallegacyadvisers.com has some materials that may be useful. And of course living your life according to your beliefs is a way to demonstrate your values even without writing them down. If you're passionate about something, it shows.

GIVING BACK

Everyone has something to share. It can be as simple as a smile or being willing to listen. But you probably already give back more than you receive. Are you a volunteer? Do you help in your place of worship? Maybe you give or raise money for causes you believe in. Or you offer time with your grandchildren, a neighbor, or a friend.

There are bigger ways to give back, too. You can get involved in politics and run for office. Or fundraise. Or write op-ed articles for the newspaper. Or hold a sign or work the polls on election day. There are many causes that need help.

Can you envision your name on a building? If you have the resources, there are schools, parks, community centers, and hospital departments looking for financial support. Your alma mater or local college has naming opportunities, too—from dorms to sports facilities and academic chairs. The same is true with museums and music organizations. More modest financial contributions can put benches in parks, stars on planetarium ceilings, trees in botanical gardens, or bricks in a walkway.

If you're an art or antiques collector, there may be a museum or school that would be a grateful recipient of your collection. If you're an artist, you can give your creations away. Or you can support community arts programs by underwriting a performance or by donating time as a docent or school group chaperone.

Mentoring is a fantastic way to give back. Use your expertise to prepare others to follow in your footsteps, whether it's teaching knitting or guiding someone through the intricacies of starting a new business. The bond that can develop will last well beyond the scope of the project. An optimistic approach and good rapport are essential elements for a good mentoring relationship.

After thirty-eight years, Elise was happy to retire from teaching English in the Los Angeles school system. But she missed being around young people. She discovered WriteGirl, a writing mentoring program for Los Angeles high school students. The program's goals include improving writing skills in all genres—fiction, scriptwriting, journalism, songwriting, nonfiction, and poetry. The program also helps with college prep for a population that traditionally did not see college as an option. This seemed like a perfect fit, and Elise applied.

Now she meets monthly with her mentee to give encouragement and editorial help. Elise knows she's inspired many of her students over the years, but the personal connection with her mentee feels special.

If you don't know of any mentoring programs, you can contact Big Brothers Big Sisters of America. With locations in most major cities, they're always looking for mentors.

WRITING YOUR OBITUARY

"Why would I want to?" you ask. Because it's the last chance for you to tell the world the story you want them to know. Why leave it to others to get it right?

The obituary is a concise life review. Writing it allows you to reflect on your life and—I hope—come to the realization that it's been complex and rewarding. Even if you'd planned to write a best-selling novel or have one of your quilts hang in a museum and those things didn't happen, you will be able to see your accomplishments. Were you a loving spouse? A doting aunt? An excellent cook? Write what makes you feel good about who you are and who you've been.

It can be a challenging task. As with any writing, avoid clichés and aim for vivid detail. You can include humor and add twists and turns to your tale. In fact, it can be like a short novel.

What to include? Name, naturally; age, date, and location of death (to be added by someone else at the time, of course); schools attended and any military service; marriages, children, and grandchildren; and awards and honors are the basics. Hobbies or interests tell a lot about you. Did anything out of the ordinary happen in your life? What inspired you? What made you laugh? How do you want to be remembered?

But don't just make a list of the details; tell a story. You can inspire others with the story of your life, when well told. Capture your essence—what makes you *you*? If you're feeling really inspired, you can write your eulogy and plan your funeral, too.

DISTRIBUTING YOUR ASSETS

Typically, we think about legacy as deciding where our money and belongings go after our death. It sounds simple, but it can become complex and emotional.

Let's start with the money. Perhaps the best plan is to give away your assets while you're still living. This lets you shrink your estate and allows you to test how your beneficiaries respond. If, for instance, you give $10,000 to a twenty-one-year-old grandson and he immediately goes to Vegas and squanders it all, you may decide to put an age restriction on any further distributions, say thirty-five, when you hope he'll be more responsible. Or maybe he decides to pay down his student loan. You'll feel fine without making any stipulations. Currently you can give $14,000 a year to an individual without incurring gift taxes. But you might need some other legal documents to distribute your wealth.

We've talked about wills in the chapter on finance. One additional point, beyond working with legal and financial professionals, is to stipulate distribution as a percentage and not a dollar amount. That way all beneficiaries will receive something if you need to use up more of your assets than you'd planned. Otherwise, with a dollar designation, some beneficiaries may empty the pot and there wouldn't be enough money to go around.

Life insurance policies and IRAs can be left via beneficiary designation to avoid probate, which can tie up funds for a year or more. Annuities can be a little more complex, but also can be managed outside the will. Obviously, every case is different, so work with professionals to make the right choices.

Do you need a trust? Like a will, a trust can stipulate how you want your assets distributed. It can also help you to avoid probate and possibly reduce your taxes, and can be a more efficient way to distribute your assets. And unlike a probated will, which is available to the public view, a trust is a private document.

Trusts are very flexible, with advantages and disadvantages to each type. Basically, there are living trusts, set up while you are alive, and testamentary trusts, outlined in your will and created at your death and which may be subject to probate. Living trusts can be revocable or irrevocable. A revocable trust lets you use your money or change the terms of the trust at any time. There are special designations for trusts that benefit a spouse, that bypass a spouse to take advantage of federal estate tax exemptions, or that skip a generation. A charitable remainder trust allows the owner to receive income for a specific time period, with the unspent balance used as a gift to the charity of her choice.

If you have a net worth over $100,000, own real estate, and have clear ideas about how you want your assets distributed, you probably would benefit from a trust. If you want your grandchildren or a charity to receive the cash, then a trust is the best way to achieve this.

To be sure you're maximizing the distributions and minimizing the taxes, consult with an estate professional. Some distributions have greater tax consequences than others, especially from IRAs, and beneficiaries' tax brackets will affect the actual amount they receive. You may, in fact, leave unequal portions of your assets that will end up being equalized by the recipient's tax situation. It becomes obvious that distribution schemes need to be revisited over time as individual circumstances, as well as tax codes, change.

Diane had retired from a career as an organic chemistry professor and wanted her legacy to continue at the college where she'd spent most of her life. She met with the development officer and arranged to fund a scholarship for a woman interested in a career in chemistry. She set up a remainder trust and used the current proceeds to fund the scholarship and give her a nice tax deduction. In this way, she was able to meet the women who were chosen, a great thrill as she became an informal mentor to several. On her death, the dollar amounts from the remainder trust will increase significantly and, as Diane has specified, will fund additional scholarships in her name.

We've talked about the money distribution, now it's time to think about the physical stuff. These can be the items that make your family unique. Mementos and heirlooms can be reminders of past relationships. Those red-and-white plastic chef-styled salt and pepper shakers bring up the story of how Grandpa George always started his menu planning with the condiment tray: green and black olives, homemade watermelon pickles, and pepperoncini. It didn't matter if it was hot dogs with all the fixings or a sliced ham buffet, the condiments were always discussed first. You've told the story so often that even your grandchildren roll their eyes when you put the salt and pepper shakers on the table and begin, "You know, my Grandpa George . . ."

But not everyone may be interested in your possessions. It's important to check with the potential recipients to find out their preferences. You might face a complicated division, such as splitting the beach house three ways when one of the children can't afford her share of the taxes and upkeep but the other two can't afford to buy her out. A better solution may be selling the house and splitting the proceeds. Discussing the options with everyone will certainly help when it comes to making a decision.

Your real gift can be giving things away, so that arguments will be kept to a minimum after your death. Communicate—one-on-one and as a group. One heir might love the idea of caring for the family collection of Hummel figurines, or no one might want them. Find out ahead of time, so that nobody is stuck with items that will only take up storage space (or end up on eBay). If you find it's best to sell or give away Aunt Jean's seventy-two-piece Limoges china, look to antique stores for buyers. There are online brokers for crystal, silver, and china. Check replacements.com. Vinyl records have become popular again, so there may be a home with a loving collector for all those Beatles and Led Zeppelin albums. Google "military donations" to find museums near you that might be interested in your war memorabilia. The same goes for photos and movies that a local historical society would treasure. Furniture and home furnishings can be donated to Habitat for Humanity's ReStore, Vietnam Veterans of America, and local organizations that provide housing for the homeless or disabled.

How do you decide to make the distributions for coveted items, like the leather-bound book collection, the piano, or art, for example? After chatting with the potential recipients about their wants, you can also have an organized giveaway where disputed items are chosen by lottery. Whatever way you decide to distribute your things, it's important to include a signed and dated memorandum with your will, providing specific details on how to divvy up your stuff. The recipients may not be happy with your decisions, but with luck they won't be angry with one another. Of course, as with cash or stock, you can give away your possessions while you're alive to see the recipients' joy.

Mary Alice, seventy-three, never married and has no children. Her estate includes some decades-old clothing found in trunks in the barn when her house was cleaned out to be sold. She didn't want to give the items to the local high school drama department, as she thought they might be worth something. She checked online for people interested in vintage clothing and discovered that the Richmond, Virginia, historical society was having an auction to renovate their building. Mary Alice contacted them and was able to donate the clothing for a sizable tax deduction. The museum's advertising and auction booklet featured a dress and straw bonnet from her donation as the cover art. She was thrilled that her grandmother's heirlooms could end up as a prized donation. The buyer, a Hollywood costume company, wanted them as models for creating day dresses from the Gilded Age.

Your legacy is one way you can achieve immortality, at least within your family and community. You will be appreciated long after you're gone if you plan ahead and make wise decisions about your legacy.

YOUR DIGITAL LEGACY

Currently, you need a court order to gain access to a deceased person's digital accounts. Your smartphone, social media, and other accounts all require user IDs and passwords. You can help by organizing your account information and keeping a copy with your will, so that your heirs and executor can have immediate access. There are digital lockbox services that you can use as well, with access via one master password.

Don't ignore your digital accounts. Your estate will continue being billed until they are closed. Make that task easier by having the information readily available. Check your state's digital estate planning laws for details.

13 ACT YOUR AGE

Being told to "act your age" is always negative. It's referencing the behavior of someone younger. It's bad for all ages: "you're too young" can be just as detrimental as "you're too old." Normal behavior at any age is a range. An eight-year-old may be skipping, reading a book, or climbing a tree. A seventy-year-old may be dancing a tango, playing bridge, or sitting quietly and knitting. Whatever you're doing at any age is "acting your age" based on your interests and abilities. Just because one sixty-five-year-old has arthritis that limits her motion doesn't mean another sixty-five-year-old can't run a race or play a full round of golf. We all should be encouraged to do what we can, and what we want, at any age. But ageism is real. And it can be limiting.

Dr. Robert N. Butler coined the term "ageism" in the late 1960s. As a psychiatrist and gerontologist, he recognized discrimination against the elderly and called it ageism. While ageism could be applied to any age group—for instance, by implying that someone is too young and inexperienced for a particular job or task—the term generally is recognized as referring to elderly people. What does ageism imply? Butler, who went on to become the founding director of the National Institute on Aging, part of the National Institutes of Health (NIH), helped answer that question by doing research on geriatric individuals. He wrote *Why Survive? Being Old in America* and *The Longevity Revolution* to share his findings.

Butler might be credited with generating widespread awareness of the issue, which continues to attract public attention. The current political situation implies that seniors are dependent and are using up resources via Medicare, Medicaid, and Social Security. While some are, others remain independent and self-sufficient, vital consumers with much to offer.

Most people want to be self-sufficient as long as possible, and they want to stay active, interact with family and friends, and have fun. But the cultural view of aging seems to treat it as a process of deterioration, dependency, and incompetence. Is that how you want to be viewed, regardless of your age? I don't. Ageism is insidious in our culture and it's especially evident in the language:

"I'm having a senior moment."

"Don't you think that outfit's a little young for you?"

"Can you remember that, or should I write it down?"

I'm sure we all find ourselves saying these things on occasion. If we want to change the acceptance of older members of society, we need to be mindful of how we contribute to the perception of ageism. We don't need to add to the stereotypes.

We all have ageist biases. Some are so ingrained that we don't even recognize them. Jokes about old people are pervasive in our culture, as one example. I'm even guilty of telling some! TV shows often depict the older members of the cast as scatter-brained, blustering, or intrusive —*Everybody Loves Raymond* and *Seinfeld* for example, and more recently, *The Millers*, *The New Normal* (both canceled after one season), and *Modern Family*. *Grace and Frankie* (Netflix), on the other hand, shows older women making a difference and really living their lives adapting to new circumstances. *Last Tango in Halifax* and *Downton Abbey* (PBS) are other TV programs that show older people in a positive light. It's interesting to note that none of these shows are on the national TV stations.

Ever since we were children, we've been hearing and seeing via the media that older people need wheelchairs, don't eat properly, and require additional liquid nutrition, have to wear adult diapers, and need lots of medication, or funeral insurance. Where is the sports car ad with a gray-haired driver? Or the commercial for pet food with a white-haired pet owner? Doesn't anyone older than forty know how to buy and use a cell phone or cable TV? These subtle but persistent images of activities showing only young or middle-aged actors in "normal" scenes, but needy or decrepit actors in others, sends the message that older individuals are diminished and need lots of help. Wrinkle cream ads show much younger models, who probably have clear skin, as the ideal to strive for. Why? My wrinkles came with a lot of life experience. Shouldn't they be acknowledged, if not celebrated, rather than erased to make me look younger?

One of the most challenging issues of ageism is that it is perceived as applying to everyone in society. This denies our individuality, which then limits the choices we have based on our needs and desires. This is as true for teens as for over-sixties. Sometimes ageism shows up as a fear of getting older, and it's easier to fall back into the stereotypes and the misperceptions, so that we don't challenge ourselves beyond our comfort zones. At any age it's important for our brain health, our psychological health, and our physical health that we be willing to try new things. Keep exercising, take chances, and be involved. This is the time to take that second chance to do what you wanted when you were younger: enroll in the course you didn't take in college, take up the musical instrument you never played, or make the trip you've long desired. We have to get rid of a mindset about what we can and can't do as we age.

"Act your age" is based on expectations of what someone should or should not be able to do at any particular age. Of course, you thought sixty was old when you were twenty-three, but now that you're sixty-seven, eighty may still seem young. As individuals, we need to be aware of what we can and can't do, but as a society we also need to have the political and social structures to support what we need. If there is a belief that old people are all alike and that they all have the same behavior, needs, and desires, then choices for all of us in housing, transportation, and health care will be limited. If old people are viewed as a burden and not as contributors to society, then many of the programs and opportunities that are available will be closed to older people.

Accepting a range of behaviors and needs, on the other hand, allows us to acknowledge and accept the contributions that we can make as vibrant older women. Making us all the same discriminates against us as individuals. When someone says, "You look great for your age," that use of "for your age" implies that you're not fitting the norm. Answering with, "What should I look like at this age?" calls into question ageist assumptions.

In her book, *This Chair Rocks: A Manifesto against Ageism*, Ashton Applewhite suggests that we become old-persons-in-training. That way we recognize that we will be old sometime in the future, and training for it means that we can make mistakes when trying new things. If we stumble along the way, that's all right; nobody is expected to be perfect while in training. We've never been this age before and we don't know who we're going to be, so we should just appreciate who we are and who we've been.

As we are getting older, we may well also become elders. In some cultures, and in previous times, elders were revered for their knowledge. They were repositories of information about the culture and certain skills that needed to be passed on to younger people; they were mentors. In many senses, we have lost that elder role in society. I think it's possible to reawaken it, even though our culture is focused more on young people and middle-aged journeys. We have become somewhat invisible, but we can embrace the marketplace and demand what we want and need. We cannot wait for people to give us that acknowledgment. We gain elder status when we volunteer with children, teach a craft or a skill, provide insight, or lead groups. When we help younger people improve their lives and encourage their visions, we become elders. But we still should remain like children, with a sense of wonder and excitement about things in life, rather than complain. We should not withdraw, but remain vital in our communities. No one will worry how old you are, and you will be "acting your age."

OVERCOMING AGEISM

Stay involved as much as you can.

Have a positive attitude.

Don't complain.

Say something if you feel you've been mistreated.

Be as independent as you can, but ask for help when you need it.

Interact with younger people.

Share your wisdom.

Celebrate who you've become and don't bemoan who you were.

CHAPTER RESOURCES

1. MATURING WITH MOXIE

ONLINE

Senior Planet website: Information and resources for aging with attitude. seniorplanet.org

Sixty+Me blog: Online community of women over sixty. sixty andme.com

Time Goes By blog: What it's really like to get old—one woman's opinions. timegoesby.net

BOOKS

Cannon, Jan. *Now What Do I Do? The Woman's Guide to a New Career.* Sterling, VA: Capital Books, 2005.

Hill, Robert. *Seven Stages for Positive Aging.* New York: Norton, 2008.

Loe, Meika. *Aging Our Way.* New York: Oxford University Press, 2011.

2. WHO ARE YOU?

ONLINE

Life Reimagined website: Part of AARP. lifereimagined.org

BOOKS

Arrien, Angeles. *Living in Gratitude.* Louisville, CO: Sounds True, 2011.

Carstensen, Laura. *A Long Bright Future.* New York: PublicAffairs, 2011.

Cowan, Rachel. *Wise Aging.* Springfield, NJ: Behrman House, 2015.

Cruikshank, Margaret. *Learning to Be Old.* Lanham, MD: Rowman and Littlefield, 2013.

Delany, Sarah Louise, Annie Elizabeth Delany, and Amy Hill Hearth. *Having Our Say.* New York: Dell, 1994.

Goldman, Connie. *Who Am I—Now That I'm Not Who I Was?* Cambridge, MN: Nodin, 2009.

Lustbader, Wendy. *Life Gets Better.* New York: Penguin, 2011.

Pevny, Ron. *Conscious Living, Conscious Aging.* New York: Adria Books, 2014.

Sarton, May. *The House by the Sea.* New York: Norton, 1995.

Thomas, Bill. *Second Wind.* New York: Simon and Schuster, 2014.

3. WORKING 9 TO 5?

ONLINE

BizBuySell website: Information about buying and selling a business. bizbuysell.com

Catalyst website: Information about inclusion for women in the workplace. catalyst.org

Encore website: Opportunities for older people to use their talents and skills. encore.org

eVirtual Services website: Online services to help with all business needs. evirtualservices.com

Experience Works website: Helping low income, unemployed, over fifty-five people look for a job. experienceworks.org

Grants website: Search and apply for grants online. grants.gov

Indiegogo website: Raise money for your business idea. indiegogo.com

Kelly Services website: Consulting, outsourcing, and part-time employment information and applications. kellyservices.com

Kickstarter website: For artists, musicians, designers, and other creative types to get funding they need to see their projects become reality. kickstarter.com

Kiva website: Lends small amounts to women in small businesses to help them succeed. kiva.org

Legal Zoom website: Information and forms for all legal needs— business, wills, intellectual property. legalzoom.com

Life Reimagined website: Part of AARP. lifereimagined.org

NextAvenue blog: Daily information about issues that are important as we age. nextavenue.org

Retirement Jobs website: Job postings and career information. retirementjobs.com

Small Business Administration website: Government site with information and forms for starting a small business. sba.gov

Seniors4Hire website: Post your résumé. seniors4hire.com

The Transition Network website: A community of women over fifty making changes in their lives. thetransitionnetwork .org

UpWork website: Hire or become a freelance worker. upwork .com

WorkForce 50 website: Job postings. workforce50.com

BOOKS

Cannon, Jan Smith. *Now What Do I Do?* Sterling, VA: Capital Books, 2005.

Collamer, Nancy. *Second-Act Careers.* New York: Random House, 2013.

4. RANDOM ACTS OF KINDNESS

ONLINE

AARP website: aarp.org

American Hiking Society website: Preserving hiking trails. americanhiking.org

Amnesty International website: A human rights advocacy organization. amnesty.org

Big Brothers Big Sisters website: Volunteer opportunities to help youth. bbbs.org

Earthwatch Institute website: Brings citizens and scientists together on environmental projects. earthwatch.org

Environmental Alliance for Senior Involvement website: Citizen involvement in environmental projects. easi.org

Experience Corps website: Part of AARP. experiencecorps.org

Global Volunteers website: Community-development projects around the world. globalvolunteers.org

Great Old Broads for Wilderness website: Preserve and protect wilderness sites. greatoldbroads.org

Generations United website: Intergenerational collaboration to support children, youth, and older citizens. gu.org

Habitat for Humanity website: Building projects in United States and abroad. habitat.org

Humane Society of United States website: Animal protection organization. humanesociety.org

Idealist website: Job postings and volunteer opportunities for people who want to make the world a better place. idealist.org

Mentor website: National mentoring partnership. mentoring.org

National Park Service website. nps.gov/volunteer

Passport in Time Forest Service website: Volunteer for environment and historic research on public lands. passportintime.com

Peace Corps website. peacecorps.gov

Points of Light website: Organization dedicated to volunteer service. pointsoflight.org

ProLiteracy website: Teach an adult to read. proliteracy.org

Red Cross website. redcross.org

Senior Corps website: Helping seniors help America. seniorcorps.org

Service Leader website: How to build better nonprofit organizations. serviceleader.org

Sierra Club website. sierraclub.org

United Nations Educational, Scientific, and Cultural Organization website. unesco.org

International Volunteer Programs Association website. volunteerinternational.org

Volunteer Match website: Matching service for volunteers and organizations. volunteermatch.org

Wilderness Volunteers website: Hands-on stewardship of public lands. wildernessvolunteers.org

WorldTeach website: Provides volunteer teachers to promote local and global citizenship. worldteach.org

BOOKS

Alboher, Marci. *The Encore Handbook.* New York: Workman Publishing, 2013.

5. A ROOF OVER YOUR HEAD

ONLINE

Age in Place website: Resource for housing and care needs. ageinplace.org

Aging in Place website: Information about aging in place. aginginplace.org

Beacon Hill Village website: Boston area NORC. beaconhillvillage. org

Cohousing Association of the United States website: Information about cohousing. cohousing.org

Eden Alternative website: Nonprofit with information about quality of life. edenalt.com

International Living website: Information about best places to live. internationalliving.com

NextAvenue website: Daily content on issues that matter to seniors. nextavenue.org

Pioneer Network website: Advocates for eldercare. pioneernetwork.net

Retirement Living Information Center website: Planning tools for retirement. retirementliving.com

RetireNet website: Information about retirement communities. retirenet.com

Senior Resource website: Housing resources. seniorresource .com

Sharing Housing website: Information about finding roommates. sharinghousing.com

Sperling's Best Places website: Comparisons of cities. bestplaces. net

US Census Bureau website: Facts and data about communities. factfinder.census.gov

USC Center for Gerontology website: HomeMods.org

USC Gerontology Center website: HomeMods.org

UTNE Reader website: Information about senior housing choices: utne.com/housing

Village to Village Network website: Information about setting up a village. vtvnetwork.org

BOOKS

Jameson, Marni. *Downsizing the Family Home.* New York: Sterling, 2016.

Pluhar, Annamarie. *Sharing Housing,* 2nd ed. East Dummerston, VT: Homemate Publishing, 2013.

6. DOLLARS AND SENSE: PLANNING FOR UNCERTAIN TIMES

ONLINE

Bankrate website: Calculators for all financial information. bankrate.com/calculators.aspx

Budget worksheets: Kiplinger.com, getsmarteraboutmoney.ca, mint.com, bankrate.com, USA Today, CNN Money

Calculators: Vanguard, T. Rowe Price, Fidelity, AARP, Analyzenow.com

Financial Planning Association website: plannersearch.org

Intuit Mint website: Budgeting information. mint.com

National Elder Law Foundation website: Find an elder law practitioner. nelf.org

National Retirement Planning Coalition website: Retirement planning. retireonyourterms.org

National Reverse Mortgage Lenders Association network: Information about reverse mortgages. reversemortgage.org

Social Security website. socialsecurity.gov

Social Security Estimator website: How to determine your SSA benefits. ssa.gov/estimator/

Women's Institute for a Secure Retirement website: Information and advocacy for women and finances. wiserwomen.org

Long-Term Care Insurance:
Genworth Financial website: LTC insurance provider. genworth.com

Life Happens website: LTC information. lifehappens.org

National Association of Health Underwriters website: Locate LTC insurance providers. NAHU.org

National Association of Insurance and Financial Advisors website: Find an agent for LTC and other insurance. NAIFA.org

Retirement Planning Tools:

Analyze Now website: analyzenow.com

CNN Money website: money.cnn.com

Fidelity Investments website: fidelity.com

Kiplinger magazine website: kiplinger.com

Ontario Securities Commission website: getsmartaboutmoney.ca

T. Rowe Price website: troweprice.com

Vanguard website: vanguard.com

BOOKS

Altman, Nancy, and Eric Kingston. *Social Security Works.* New York: New Press, 2015.

7. FAMILY (AND OTHER RELATIVE MATTERS)

ONLINE

Eldercare Locator website: Find local care resources. eldercare.gov

Family Caregiver Alliance website: Information, support, and resources for caregivers. caregiver.org

National Alliance for Caregiving website: Coalition of family caregiving organizations focusing on research and advocacy. caregiving.org

BOOKS

Aronson, Wendy. *Refeathering the Empty Nest*. Lanham, MD: Rowan and Littlefield, 2016.

Nemzoff, Ruth. *Don't Bite Your Tongue*. New York: MacMillan, 2008.

———. *Don't Roll Your Eyes*. New York: MacMillan, 2012.

Taylor, Roberta and Dorian Mintzer. *The Couple's Retirement Puzzle*. Naperville, IL: Source Books, 2014.

8. MAKE NEW FRIENDS, BUT KEEP THE OLD

ONLINE

Big and Beautiful Singles website. bbpeoplemeet.com

Black Singles website. blacksingles.com

Catholic Match website. catholicmatch.com

Christian Mingle website. christianmingle.com

Dating for Seniors website. datingforseniors.com

eHarmony website. eharmony.com

FirstMet website. firstmet.com

Foreign Datefinder website. foreigndatefinder.com

JDate website: Jewish focused. jdate.com

LoveAccess website. loveaccess.com

Match.com website. match.com

MeetUp website: Meet people with similar interests in your area. meetup.com

OKcupid website. OKcupid.com

OurTime website: Over-fifty dating site. ourtime.com

Right Stuff Introduction Service website: Ivy League dating service. rightstuffdating.com

SeniorFriendFinder website: Dating for older singles. seniorfriendfinder.com

SeniorMatch website: Dating site for those over fifty. seniormatch.
com

SeniorPeopleMeet website. seniorpeoplemeet.com

SeniorsMeet website. seniorsmeet.com

SilverSingles website: Community for mature singles.
silversingles.com

SingleParentMeet website. singleparentmeet.com

The Three Tomatoes website: Resource for older women in NYC
and LA. thethreetomatoes.com

Virtual Dating Assistants website: Dating site.
virtualdatingassistants.com

BOOKS

Anderson, Joan. *A Walk on the Beach.* New York: Broadway Books,
2005.

Drabble, Margaret. *The Seven Sisters.* New York: Mariner Books,
2003.

Heyman, Arlene. *Scary Old Sex.* New York: Bloomsbury, 2016.

Lachs, Mark, MD. *Treat Me, Not My Age.* Penguin: New York,
2010.

Nelson, John E., and Richard N. Bolles. *What Color is Your
Parachute? For Retirement, 2nd Ed.* Ten Speed: Emeryville, CA,
2010.

Price, Joan. *Better Than I Ever Expected.* Berkeley, CA: Seal Press,
2005.

——. *Naked at Our Age.* Berkeley, CA: Seal Press,
2011.

Trafford, Abigail. *As Time Goes By.* New York: Basic Books, 2009.

9. IF YOU HAVE YOUR HEALTH . . .

ONLINE

Alcoholics Anonymous. aa.org

Aging with Dignity website: Advocates for end-of-life care. agingwithdignity.org

Alzheimer's Association website. alz.org

American Geriatrics Society website: Information about healthy aging. healthinaging.org

American Heart Association website. americanheart.org

American Society on Aging website: Resources for those working with and for older adults. asaging.org

American Stroke Association website. strokeassociation.org

Calm website: Online meditation. calm.com

Centers for Disease Control and Prevention website: Health information for older adults. cdc.gov/aging

HealthWatch 360 website: Track food, exercise, and health symptoms. healthwatch360.com

Mayo Clinic website. mayoclinic.org

Medicaid website. medicaid.gov

Medicare website. medicare.gov

National Center for Complementary and Integrative Health website: Information about alternative medicine. nccam.nih .gov

National Center for Quality Assurance website: Concerned with health care quality. ncqa.org

National Institute on Aging website. nia.nih.gov/health

National Hospice and Palliative Care Organization website: Information for end-of-life care. caringinfo.org

Office of Disease Prevention and Health Promotion website: Prevention and wellness information. health.gov

Office of Women's Health website: Focused on improving the health of girls and women. womenshealth.gov

Our Bodies Ourselves website: Information on women's reproductive health and sexuality. ourbodiesourselves.org

thirdAGE website: Health and wellness site for women over forty-five. thirdage.com

US Health and Human Services website: Eldercare locator. eldercare.gov

Yoga Glo website: Online yoga and meditation. yogaglo.com

BOOKS

Gawande, Atul. *Being Mortal.* New York: Metropolitan Books, 2014.

Lacks, Mark. *What Your Doctor Won't Tell You About Getting Older.* New York: Penguin, 2011.

Raty, John J. *Spark: The Revolutionary New Science of Exercise and the Brain.* New York: Little, Brown, 2008.

10. BRAIN GYM

ONLINE

AdventureWomen website: Adventure travel tours for active women thirty-five and older. adventurewomen.com

Backroads website: Active travel vacations. backroads.com

BrainHq website: Online brain games. brainhq.com

Broadway Fantasy Camp website. broadwayfancamp.com

Chautauqua Institution website: Lectures and sermons from Chautauqua, New York. greatlecturelibrary.com

Center for Furniture Craftsmanship website: Woodworking classes in Maine. woodschool.org

Chicago Mosaic School website: Courses in mosaics. chicagomosaicschool.com

Clay Studio website: Ceramics courses. theclaystudio.org

Cornell University Viticulture and Enology website: Courses on winemaking. sce.cornell.edu/ps/cuvee

CreativeLive website: Courses in creative endeavors. creativelive. com

Creativity Workshop website: Online courses on creativity. creativityworkshop.com

Crow Canyon Archeological Center website: Hands-on experience in archeological research. crowcanyon.org

Culinary Institute of America website: Cooking courses. enthusiasts.ciachef.edu/boot-camps/

Ed2Go website: Online courses. ed2go.com

edX website: Free online courses. edx.org

Flying Colors Art Workshops website. flyingcolorsart.com

Genco website: Games for adults. genco-games.com

Gotham Writers Workshop website: Online writing courses. writingclasses.com

Hanoi Cooking Centre website: Vietnamese cooking classes. hanoicookingcentre.com

HomeExchange website. homeexchange.com

Idyllwild Arts: Residential arts high school and summer programs for all ages. idyllwildarts.org

Institute for Learning in Retirement (various)

International Center of Photography website: Courses. icp.org

Joseph Van Os Photo Safaris website: Photography travel. photosafaris.com

National Center for Creative Aging website: Resources for creative expression. creativeaging.org

Natural Gourmet Institute website: Cooking classes. naturalgourmetinstitute.com

Osher Lifelong Learning Institutes website. osher.net

Penland School of Crafts website: penland.org

The Pit: People's Improv Theater website: Improv classes in New York city. thepit-nyc.com

Rent Villas website: European villa rentals. rentvillas.com

RoadScholar website: Experiential learning in United States and abroad. roadscholar.org

Sanibel Island Writers Conference website. fgcu.edu/siwc/

Santa Fe Writers Conference website. santafewritersconference .com

School of Artisan Food website: Cooking courses. schoolofartisanfood.org

Second City website: Improv and comedy-writing classes for adults. secondcity.com

SeniorNet website: Courses on computer technology. seniornet .org

Shenandoah Art Destination website: Art courses. shenandoahartdestination.com

SilverSea website: Cruises. silversea.com

Snow Farm website: New England craft program. snowfarm.org

Taos Art School website. taosartschool.org

Thousand Islands Art Center: Preserves the skills of traditional artists and artisans. tiartscenter.org

Tripping website: Vacation rentals. tripping.com

Two Bordelais website: Food, wine, and cooking classes in France. twobordelais.com

Udemy website: Online learning. udemy.com

Virtual Senior Center website: Connect with other seniors online for learning and games. vdcm.selfhelp.net

BOOKS

Carstensen, Laura. *A Long Bright Future.* New York: Broadway Books, 2009.

Cohen, Gene. *The Mature Mind.* New York: Basic Books, 2005.

Goldberg, Natalie. *Writing Down the Bones.* Boulder, CO: Shambala Books, 2005.

Vickers, Salley. *Miss Garnet's Angel.* New York: Plume, 2002.

11. WE'RE IN THIS TOGETHER

ONLINE

AARP website. aarp.org

Alliance for Aging Research website: Advocacy organization on aging. agingresearch.org

Changing Aging website: Source for information about aging research. changingaging.org

Conscious Elders Network website: Social and economic justice advocates. consciouselders.org

Elders Climate Action website: Advocates for climate change and understanding. eldersclimateaction.org

Emily's List website: Supporting pro-choice Democratic women candidates. emilyslist.org

Facebook. facebook.com

Instagram. instagram.com

League of Women Voters website. lwv.org

National Council on Aging website: Advocacy group supporting the health and economic security of older adults. ncoa.org

National Partnership for Women and Families website: Advocacy group supporting issues that relate to women and families. nationalpartnership.org

National Federation of Republican Women website: Recruit, train, and elect Republican women. nfrw.org

National Organization for Women website: Feminist grassroots activists. now.org

Peace Corps website. peacecorps.gov

Senior Corps website: Senior volunteer opportunities.
seniorcorps.org

Senior Something website: Directory of information on other
sites. seniorsomething.com

Skype. skype.com

The Transition Network website: Networking site for
women over fifty who are making changes in their lives.
thetransitionnetwork.com

12. LIFE'S LEFTOVERS: YOUR LEGACY

ONLINE

Ancestry website: Genealogy and DNA testing for ancestry.
ancestry.com

Charity Navigator website: Rates charities. charitynavigator.com

Everplans website: Digital archives. everplans.com

Grandparent information website: Ideas and connections for
grandparents and surrogate grandparents: grandparents.org

GuideStar website: Information on nonprofits. guidestar.com

Personal Legacy website: personallegacyadvisors.com

23andMe website: DNA testing for ancestry and health. 23andme.
com

US Funerals Online website: Funeral guide and funeral home
directory. us-funerals.com

US Living Will Registry website: Online database for storing
advance directives. uslivingwillregistry.com

BOOKS

Butler, Robert N., MD. *The Longevity Revolution.* New York: Public
Affairs, 2008.

———. *Why Survive? Being Old in America.* Baltimore: Johns
Hopkins University Press, 2002.

Goldberg, Natalie. *Old Friend from Far Away: The Practice of Writing Memoir.* New York: Free Press, 2007.

O'Faolain, Nuala. *My Dream of You.* New York: Riverhead Books, 2002.

13. ACT YOUR AGE

ONLINE

Pass It On Network website: Conversation about issues arising from living longer. passitonnetwork.org

Sage-ing International website: Conversations honoring the aging process. sage-ing.org

This Chair Rocks blog: Conversations about ageism. thischairrocks.com

BOOKS

Applewhite, Ashton. *This Chair Rocks: A Manifesto against Ageism.* New York: Networked Books, 2016

Bateson, Mary Catherine. *Composing a Further Life.* New York: Knopf, 2010.

Guillette, Margaret Morganroth. *Agewise.* Chicago: University of Chicago Press, 2010.

Karpf, Anne. *How to Age.* New York: Macmillan, 2014

INDEX

Note: Page numbers in *italics* indicate tables or figures.

ABOUT THE AUTHOR

Jan Cannon, PhD, is the author of *Now What Do I Do? The Woman's Guide to a New Career* (Capital Books, 2005). Jan has spent more than twenty years helping clients find new jobs, start new businesses, or plan for their retirement. Recently, her coaching business has evolved into an online, interactive coaching program that serves English-speaking clients throughout the world.

Articles about Jan have appeared in the *Wall Street Journal*, *Business 2.0*, *Real Simple*, *Women's World*, *AARP Bulletin*, *Working Mother*, and other publications. She has served as an online expert with CIO.com, jobfindtoday.com, and WomenWork.org, and she writes content for Job-Hunt.org. Her blog, maturingwithmoxie.com, offers information about the issues women face as they age.

Jan lectures and leads workshops on planning for life after sixty, making career choices, and networking. She and Rev. Jennifer Cook work together providing workshops and retreats on personal renewal.